EXPERIENTIAL EXERCISES

IN

HUMAN RESOURCE MANAGEMENT

CAROL A. SALES
Brock University

FRANCES A. OWEN
Niagara University

MARY ANN LESPERANCE
Marshall & Company

Prentice Hall Canada Inc., Scarborough, Ontario

Prentice-Hall, Inc., Upper Saddle River, New Jersey
Prentice-Hall International (UK) Limited, London
Prentice-Hall of Australia, Pty. Limited, Sydney
Prentice-Hall Hispanoamericana, S.A., Mexico City
Prentice-Hall of India Private Limited, New Delhi
Prentice-Hall of Japan, Inc., Tokyo
Simon & Schuster Southeast Asia Private Limited, Singapore
Editora Prentice-Hall do Brasil, Ltda., Rio de Janeiro

ISBN 0-13-021805-7

Publisher and Editorial Director: Patrick Ferrier
Acquisitions Editor: Mike Ryan
Senior Marketing Manager: Ann Byford
Developmental Editor: Sherry Torchinsky
Production Editor: Mary Ann McCutcheon
Production Coordinator: Janette Lush
Cover Design: Julia Hall, Monica Kompter
Cover Image: Photodisk

1 2 3 4 5   04 03 02 01 00

Printed and bound in Canada

Visit the Prentice Hall Canada Web site! Send us your comments, browse our catalogues, and more. **www.phcanada.com** Or reach us through e-mail at **phcinfo_pubcanada@prenhall.com**

DEDICATION

To   Betty Sales
      and
      Jane and Betty Jean Lavallee (C.A.S.)

To   F. George-Ann Owen
      and
      In memory of John V. Owen (F.A.O.)

To   My son, Marshall, for keeping me light-hearted and grounded (M.A.L.)

TABLE OF CONTENTS

PREFACE

Human Resource Management is a dynamic profession that is changing rapidly in response to new trends in research and practice. These exercises have been developed to introduce students to some of the experiences and dilemmas that face HR professionals on a day to day basis. From a constructivist perspective, these experiences will encourage students to develop their personal perspectives on a complex management function. In addition to the experiences themselves, the debriefing activities encourage students to become reflective learners.

Experiential Exercises in Human Resource Management is one of a series of three related books of experiential exercises. The other two are *Experiential Exercises in Organizational Behaviour* and *Experiential Exercises in Management.* This book has been developed with one eye firmly focused on theory and the other firmly focused on the needs of practitioners. As part of the planning process for this project, a focus group was held in Toronto with HR and senior business professionals from a variety of organizations. They were asked to discuss the major issues facing people in the field today, the skills and competencies they look for in new HR professionals in the areas of HR and Organizational Behaviour, and the pressures that are likely to arise in the foreseeable future. The results of this focus group, combined with literature from the academic and professional sectors, guided our selection of topics.

This book is organized into four parts. The exercises in Part 1 provide an Introduction to HRM for the 21st century. These include exercises that orient students to the Bigger Picture for HRM with a focus on the macro view of organizations, and exercises that introduce students to the Evolution of HRM as a management function with a focus on the reinvention of the HR function and key resources for the HR professional.

Part 2 focuses on Strategic HR Management. From HR and Organizational Trend Analysis, to HR Strategy Development, Planning, Employee Relations and Diversity, and Legal Issues in HR, this section focuses on core strategic issues for the HR function. In this section, students will have the opportunity to examine the impact of telecommuting, investigate issues related to corporate social responsibility, explore strategies that companies are using to project and maintain "cool" employment image, and reflect on ways to promote diversity in their organizations.

Part 3 spotlights HR Services Delivery. This section includes subsections that focus on Job Requirements, Recruitment and Selection, Orientation, Performance Management, HR Development, Career Development, Reward and Recognition and Health and Safety. These activities help students to grapple with the fundamental issues that face HR professionals every day: how to recruit and keep talented employees, how to provide employees with the information they need to do their jobs effectively and efficiently, how to provide both positive and negative feedback in a way that promotes employee growth, and how to keep people safe at work.

Part 4 focuses on Building Employee Commitment. The critical skills of maintaining a healthy Work/Life Balance and developing effective Communication with employees are reviewed in these exercises.

The Instructor's Manual that accompanies this book provides background and support materials that facilitate completion of the exercises.

This book will challenge students to explore the wide range of competencies and skills required by HR professionals and inspire them to develop their own perspective on the HR function. It is our fondest hope that students will have fun learning through these exercises. Any student who works through all of these exercises will have an excellent introduction to the critical role played by HR professionals in 21st century organizations and to the competencies and skills that are fundamental in this role.

ACKNOWLEDGMENTS

We are very grateful for the help and support of the team at Prentice Hall Canada in particular we would like to thank Sherry Torchinsky and Amber Wallace for their guidance and understanding. We wish to thank the HR and management professionals who shared their experience and concerns with us: Kate Wooten, The Hospital for Sick Children; Marnie Keith-Murray, Keith-Murray Partnership; Brian Flanagan, The Toronto Hospital; Jeff Lee, The Toronto Hospital; Stephen Ryan, UNUM CANADA; Christine Croucher, CIBC; Andrea Waines, Miller Dallas Inc.; and Pete Van Hezewyk, Loyalty Management Group. This book would never have been completed without the skill, good humour and endless energy and patience of Rosalie Velicevic. Her computer skills were invaluable in the completion of this book. We are also grateful to Amanda Oosterveer for the skill, good humour and patience she brought to the project wrap-up. This was truly a team effort which gave us all an opportunity to learn from one another.

Carol Sales wishes to express her gratitude to Frances Owen and Mary Ann Lesperance for their dedication to this book and for their continuing friendship and mentoring. She also wishes to thank Joel J. and Frank B. Samuels and her colleagues at Brock University, especially: Dean Martin Kusy, Ronald McTavish, Mark Thomas, Eli Levanoni, Sharon Broderick, John Barr, Margot Adams-Webber, and Jila Boal.

Frances Owen wishes to thank the other members of writing team, Carol Sales and Mary Ann Lesperance, for a wonderful learning experience. She is also grateful to her colleagues in the College of Education at Niagara University for their encouragement and good humour: Father Daniel O'Leary, Dean of Education, Dr. Robin Erwin, Chair, Drs. Salvatore Pappalardo, Jackie MacFarland, Deborah Erickson, Thomas Sheeran, Paul Vermette, Frank Calzi, Carmelo Sapone, Chandra Foote, Rita Moretti, Alice Blake-Stalker, Jennifer Wilson-Bridgman, and Delar Singh, and to Mary Anne Brown for her patience. Special thanks to Dr. Victor Owen, Sheila Moores, Jim, Julie and Evan Owen and, especially to Joel J. and Frank B. Samuels for keeping her grounded.

Mary Ann Lesperance is ever grateful to Carol Sales and Frances Owen for their leap of faith in asking her to join their team. She wishes to thank her family, professional colleagues, and friends for their input, encouragement, support, patience, and continual belief in her abilities, especially her Mom (Mary Lesperance Hulett), Victoria's parents (Lisa Craig and Peter Van Hezewyk), Brian Flanagan, Cory Hagopian, Mary Knapp, Debbie Lee, Linda Morrison, Gary and Diana Lesperance, Laurie Panchyshyn and the Grey Gables' Ladies, and her Book Club.

ACKNOWLEDGMENTS

PART 1

INTRODUCTION TO HRM FOR THE 21st CENTURY

THE BIGGER PICTURE FOR HRM

1. LET ME TELL YOU ABOUT MY JOB: ORGANIZATIONAL ART

 **LEARNING OBJECTIVES:**

1. To serve as an icebreaker for the many experiential exercises to be presented throughout this course.

2. To provide a vehicle through which you can learn more about work organizations with which you are already somewhat familiar. e.g., co-op placements and summer jobs.

3. To give you an opportunity to look at your work organization "through a fish-eye lens" and visualize for classmates a sample of the complex interpersonal interactions you have encountered.

4. To begin your personal journey of integrating course material and your own work experience.

5. To present an opportunity for you to gain an appreciation of "the bigger picture" of the organizations e.g., the micro and macro issues in people management.

TYPE OF EXERCISE:

Small group activities and class-wide discussion

RELATED CONCEPTS:

*   Micro and Macro Organizational Behaviour, Organizational Theory, and Design topics:

    *   motivation
    *   communication

- stress
- conflict and co-operation
- leadership and supervision
- control and culture
- human resource management practices
- working environment and quality of work life

 TIME: 25 minutes

Small groups will typically require a maximum of 15 minutes to complete discussion, planning and drawing their organizational art. Each group in turn will then display its "creation" and will offer a brief interpretation for the rest of the class. Class discussion will not be held until after all groups have presented their artwork. This is expected to take 2 minutes per group.

Next, the instructor and the class will discuss their interpretations and their reactions to the artwork. This part of the activity could add up to 3 minutes per group.

BACKGROUND:

Work organizations are everywhere. They come in all shapes and sizes. Some endure short, tortuous existence while others sustain long, prideful organizational lives. Some plot ambitious global treks. Others are content to stay on the home turf. Whatever their mission, size, and global reach, work organizations profoundly affect the lives of those they employ and beyond.

Your first lessons about the inner complexities of work organizations most likely came from overhearing the daily "post-mortem" analyses recounted with a fair bit of animation, if not agitation, by your parents and siblings. Later, while still at school, you may have found yourself experiencing these infamous work organizations as you were hired for part-time jobs or selected for co-op placements.

This exercise will give you the opportunity to share your insights on and feelings about the inner workings of the organization you know best.

David Cherrington[1], from whose work this exercise is adapted, offers the following illustrations as inspiration for your drawings or cartoons:

> A woman who worked in a large bureaucratic organization with rigid rules and procedures caricatured her organization as a large dinosaur sinking in a pool of quicksand which represented the rules. One of her colleagues illustrated the same idea by drawing a picture of an overweight cat entangled in a ball of twine, which represented the rules. A

3

person who worked in the formatting department of an advertising agency wrote the story about a hapless fool who was caught on a treadmill with fire-breathing dragons close behind. A union steward drew a picture of a battle scene between management and union. The company logo or union symbol on the warriors' swords and shields depicted the union's assault against the corporate castle.

 MATERIALS NEEDED:

- One sheet of flip chart paper for each small group
- One set of coloured markers (with at least 3 different colours)
- One roll of masking tape

PROCESS/INSTRUCTIONS:

1. Your instructor will divide the class into groups of four.

2. Each person in the group will describe one summer job or co-op placement (or other organizational setting) to group members within one minute each. A "fish-eye" view should be encouraged for the description.

3. Within your group, decide on the most interesting workplace and proceed to tell the story by drawing a multi-colour cartoon or writing a metaphor. Your group member who actually experienced this situation will instruct other group members on how best to illustrate it.

4. Your instructor will ask each group in turn to present its cartoon (or metaphor) to the class.

DEBRIEFING:

1. What are the common organizational themes depicted in the artwork (e.g., good management practices, bad management practices, the pressures, feelings of success)?

4

2.   Based on the course outline, or the table of contents of your text, what topics do you expect will address the common organizational themes you identified in your answer to question 1. above?

3.   What conclusions can be drawn from this exercise with respect to the importance of people management skills in today's organizations?

REFERENCE:

1.   Cherrington, D. (1989). *Organizational Behavior: The Management of Individual and Organizational Performance.* Upper Saddle River, NJ: Prentice-Hall Inc., p. 511. Reprinted by permission.

2. TOTALLY RAD:
A MEDIA SCAVENGER HUNT PORTFOLIO OF POSITIVE AND FUN TRENDS IN CONTEMPORARY ORGANIZATIONS

 LEARNING OBJECTIVES:

1. To give you an opportunity to search the media for "signs of the times" in contemporary work organizations.

2. To heighten your awareness of the many new and positive changes which are affecting the workforce.

3. To have fun doing this assignment and to create a lasting memory of this course.

TYPE OF EXERCISE:

Individual portfolio and class presentations

RELATED CONCEPTS:

- Organizational trends
- Organizational culture
- Changing workplace demographics
- Managerial practices
- Leadership
- Motivation

 TIME: 10 minutes (per student presentation distributed throughout the course)

Individual students will given a maximum of 10 minutes (or a different time limit as authorized by your instructor) to present their portfolio to the class. Your instructor will draw up a schedule of available time slots that run from the middle of the course to the end.

BACKGROUND:

There's no doubt that contemporary organizations are reeling from the dizzying twirl of change that has swept through in the last decade or so. The media, it seems, has profiled the negative side effects with painful persistence. But there is another side - a positive side to changes flooding into contemporary organizations. The younger generations which have entered the workforce over the last 10 years or so are making their presence felt and are changing the face of work in many positive ways.

This exercise will give you an opportunity to look at the interesting and fun side of working in contemporary organizations.

PREASSIGNMENT STUDENT PREPARATION:

In the first quarter of this course, your instructor will outline the requirements of this assignment for you. In essence, you will work alone outside of class to complete a portfolio of media items to show your understanding of the positive changes that are changing the face of Canadian workplaces. For a period of a few weeks, you will be searching all forms of media e.g., daily newspapers, popular business magazines, recent movies, news documentaries, televison business programs, and the Internet. Your end product, or as HR professionals call it your "deliverable" will be a collage of media items amassed in one well-designed portfolio which you will present to the class in a 10 minute time slot sometime after the mid-point of this course. Your instructor will assign the time slots (specific class day and 10 minute time slot) by lottery in the first few weeks of this course.

Your portfolio will be entitled: "The changing face of work" and must contain (at minimum) the following (unless otherwise directed by your instructor):

- five cartoons representing at least three different cartoon strips and your commentary on each;
- two references to a movie with your commentary;
- the web addresses and your summary of the sites of three Canadian companies with interesting and fun organizational cultures;
- three newspaper articles and your commentary on each;
- three articles from three different popular business magazines with your commentary on each; and
- two summaries of a Canadian business televison program (aired between six months before this course started and today) e.g., CBC's Venture, National Magazine, or Culture Shock.

In addition you might want to approach several organizations in your community to obtain a copy of interesting promotional material to display in your portfolio. Some organizations might even lend you a copy of their promotional video.

Remember your overall goal in this assignment is to showcase your knowledge of the positive side of the changing place of work. To make a final selection on any item for your portfolio, ask yourself if this item would have been likely to have appeared in the media five years ago and if this item is workplace-related, interesting and fun. If your answer is "yes", include the item in your portfolio. If your answer is "no", forget about this item. If you have fun amassing this portfolio, your classmates will enjoy listening to your presentation.

PROCESS/INSTRUCTIONS:

Present your portfolio to the class in your time slot (drawn earlier in the course by lottery).

FOLLOW-UP ACTIVITIES:

1. Invite HR professionals and other leaders and managers from organizations in your community to hear and comment on the portfolio presentations.

2. Amass a class portfolio that contains the very best items from all the portfolios and offer to present it as a part of your school's next Open House for the public or to take it to local high schools as a part of your school's high school recruitment program.

3. Keep your portfolio intact to take with you to job interviews to showcase your understanding of contemporary workplaces.

THE EVOLUTION OF HRM

3. BUSTING THE GHOSTS OF HR PAST: DISPELLING THE MYTHS OF THE HR FUNCTION

 LEARNING OBJECTIVES:

1.   To raise your awareness of the ghosts and myths that haunt the HR function from the past.

2.   To illustrate the transition from the old view of HRM to the modern view.

TYPE OF EXERCISE:

Individual activity, small group activity and class-wide discussion

RELATED CONCEPTS:

- Evolution of HRM
- HR and organizational trend analysis

 TIME: 35 minutes

The small group discussion of the myths and rewriting the new realities will typically require 10 minutes. The class-wide discussion of the rewritten myths will take another 15 minutes. The debriefing will require 10 minutes.

BACKGROUND:

The HR profession has its fair share of ghosts. Margaret Buteriss, in her book: *Reinventing HR: Changing Roles To Create the High-Performance Organization*, said: "The equation of Human Resources with the processing of personnel forms - payroll, benefits, evaluation- no longer makes sense to companies driven by global markets, global competition, and new technology".[1]

This exercise will give you the opportunity to confront and dispel many ghosts that have the HR function for far too long.

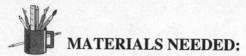 MATERIALS NEEDED:

- One copy of a list of "Old Myths" about HR for each student (to be distributed by your instructor)
- One copy of a second handout on myths for each student (to be distributed by your instructor before the end of the exercise)

PREASSIGNMENT STUDENT PREPARATION:

Before the class in which you will be discussing this exercise, your instructor will give you a list of old HR myths and will ask you to take some time to reflect on the today's realities for each myth. Be sure to bring your notes on your reflections to class.

PROCESS/INSTRUCTIONS:

1. Your instructor will divide the class into small groups and will assign one or two myths to each group for discussion. Rewrite the assigned myth(s) to reflect today's realities.

2. Your instructor will go down the list of myths one at a time and will ask the appropriate group to offer its rewritten version of the myth to reflect today's realities.

3. When all the rewritten myths have been presented in class, your instructor will distribute a second handout on the myths.

DEBRIEFING:

1.   Which myth(s) had you heard before you received the list in class?

2.   Which myth(s) surprised you the most? Please explain.

3.   What effect would you guess such myths have had on HR professionals over the years?

4.   What organizational impact(s) do you think these myths have had in the long run?

5. What new realities for HR surprised you the most? The least? Please explain your answers.

FOLLOW-UP ACTIVITIES:

1. Invite a panel of HR professionals from a number of different kinds of organizations to come to class to discuss the myths and realities.

2. Interview a retired executive (not an HR professional) from a company to test out the list of rewritten myths from the class.

REFERENCE:

1. Butteriss, B. (1998). Reinventing HR: *Changing Roles To Create The High-Performance Organization.* Toronto: John Wiley & Sons, p. 5.

4. PLANNING MY HR CAREER: IDENTIFYING HR CAREER OPPORTUNITIES

 LEARNING OBJECTIVES:

1.   To provide a vehicle through which you can explore the career opportunities for new graduates in the field of human resources.

2.   To further your understanding of the competencies currently being expected of new hires in the field of HR by various organizations.

3.   To illustrate the value of adopting a proactive stance toward career planning.

TYPE OF EXERCISE:

Small group activities, a telephone interview and class-wide discussions

RELATED CONCEPTS:

*   Career planning
*   Recruitment and selection

 TIME: 90 minutes

Small groups will typically require a maximum of 15 minutes to prepare in class for the telephone interviews. The maximum time allowed for the telephone interview is 15 minutes. The preparation of the class report is expected to take about 15 minutes. Finally, the delivery of the class report by each group and the debriefing will require another 45 minutes (depending on the number of groups).

BACKGROUND:

As you are probably already painfully aware, students who are currently specializing in HR courses face an ever-increasingly competitive marketplace as they seek employment. They can easily become overwhelmed and discouraged as they struggle to launch their career in the field of HR. Students who have little, if any, formal exposure to the real world application of the material they have been studying may have an idealized or, alternatively, a demonized view of the nature of work in the HR field for the 21st century.

This exercise will give you an opportunity to reach out from the classroom to do your own reality check on various kinds of organizations. You will be able to frame, and then ask, probing questions of practicing HR professionals about how best to gain entry into the HR field. The information you will receive will be invaluable in your HR career planning. HR professionals working in the field understand very well how crucial early and effective mentorship is to launching a career in HR.

 MATERIALS NEEDED:

- Three blank write-on overhead transparencies per group
- One washable transparency marker for each group
- Background materials on the assigned organizations

PREASSIGNMENT STUDENT PREPARATION:

Your instructor will assign you to a small group during the class which precedes the one in which you will complete this exercise. Each group will be given the name of a local organization which has an HR department (no doubt a large organization rather than a small one!) and which has agreed to participate in this exercise.

In preparation for your telephone interview with the HR professional in your assigned organization, you and your group members will attempt to learn as much as possible about your assigned organization in the time available. You will need to bring to class any written materials you can find on your organization. The local branch of the Chamber of Commerce, the Classified Section of your local newspaper(s) and/or the Internet will be very valuable in your research.

PROCESS/INSTRUCTIONS:

1. Divide into your assigned small groups. Share with your group all the written materials you have gathered on your assigned organization. As a group, get to know your organization by answering the following questions:

    - In what sector (public or private) does your organization operate?
    - How many people does it employ?
    - What is its purpose/mission?
    - Is this a domestic, transnational, international or global organization?
    - What does its organizational structure look like?
    - Where does the HR department fit in this structure?

2. Within your small group, prepare a list of six questions that your group will ask during the telephone interview with the HR contact in your assigned organization. The purpose of the questions will be to help you to discover for yourself what competencies employers' expect of their new hires in HR and what opportunities await new graduates with a specialty in human resources in the current job market. To get you started, here are a few sample questions you might consider:

    - Which entry-level position in your organization would you recommend as most helpful to a new graduate who wishes to develop a career in HR?
    - How did you launch your HR career?
    - Could you please tell us what types of assignments a new graduate in HR would be expected to complete?
    - What are the most valuable competencies a new HR graduate would need to have to launch an HR career in the 21st century?

3. Obtain the name and telephone number of your group's HR contact person from your instructor. Elect one group member to conduct the telephone interview on behalf of your group. Out of respect for your contact person, please ensure that your telephone interview does not exceed 15 minutes. Your instructor will provide a few additional helpful hints on interviewing by telephone and will explain how and when the telephone calls will be made. While the interviewer is on the telephone, the remaining members of each group will prepare a very brief overview of the assigned organization (as established in Step 1. above). Each group will obtain three blank transparency sheets and one transparency marker from your instructor. On one transparency sheet, group members will print the overview of their assigned organization. This information will be shared with the rest of the class during Step 4. below.

4. After all the telephone interviews have been completed, each group will discuss, summarize and present their interview results to the class. The interview results will be summarized on two transparency sheets. Each group will begin their report to the class with the overview of their assigned organization (as prepared in Step 3. above).

DEBRIEFING:

1. What were the similarities/differences among the competencies expected of new HR graduates across the different organizations contacted?

2. What were the similarities/differences among the types of entry-level positions recommended for new HR graduates across the different organizations contacted?

3. To what position in the hierarchy do each of the HR professionals contacted report? Why is this significant? What conclusion do you draw from this information?

4. What was the most surprising and/or unique response given by any of the HR professionals contacted? Please explain in more detail.

5.   What difference did the type of organization represented make to the responses of the different HR professionals?

FOLLOW-UP ACTIVITIES:

1.   Each group should conclude this exercise by sending a "thank you" letter to their HR contact.

2.   All or some of the groups (or individuals) may wish to summarize the results of their investigation and mail a copy to their HR contact person. Some may wish to include a request for further (voluntary) feedback from the contact person(s).

3.   With the written permission of the individuals and organizations studied in this exercise, the class may wish to prepare a paper describing their results and submit it for publication in the newsletter of a local HR association.

5. HOW ARE WE DOING?:
MEASURING THE HUMAN RESOURCE DEPARTMENT'S PERFORMANCE IN KEY RESULTS AREAS

 LEARNING OBJECTIVES:

1.   To learn the rationale for assessing the HR Department's performance as a service giver within an organization.

2.   To learn the criteria used by the HR department to assess HR's performance in key areas.

3.   To learn about measures that are appropriate for tracking HR's performance.

TYPE OF EXERCISE:

Small group activities and class-wide discussion

RELATED CONCEPTS:

- HR strategy
- HR areas of specialty

 TIME: 50 minutes

Small group activities will typically require 20 minutes. The report to the class is expected to take 20 minutes. The debriefing will require an additional 10 minutes.

BACKGROUND:

Too often in the past, personnel departments (as they were called) were seen as not adding value to the organizations. In fact, some HR departments were seen as overhead.

Clearly in the "lean and mean" era of organizations, from the 1990s on, HR departments who do not prove their contribution to the bottom-line are in great danger of being outsourced. HR departments must link their strategy to that of the organization and must be proactive in documenting the added value of their support for the organization. Feedback from HR's "internal clients" i.e., within the organization and monitoring key performance areas for the HR department will go along way toward helping HR to showcase its added value to the organization and thereby will enhance its credibility within the organization.

This exercise will give you the opportunity to learn more about the "whys" and "hows" of the HR department's imperative to prove its added value to the organization.

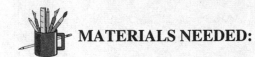 **MATERIALS NEEDED:**

- Two pieces of flip chart paper and one marker for each small group
- One roll of masking tape

PROCESS/INSTRUCTIONS:

1. Your instructor will divide the class into six groups and will assign each group one of the following HR specialties:

    - Recruitment and selection
    - HR development
    - Orientation
    - Performance management
    - HR strategy and planning
    - Reward and recognition

2. Brainstorm within your group a list of potential contributions an effective HR department can make to an organization in your assigned area of specialty.

3. Within your group, discuss the question: What are the criteria the HR department should use to assess its performance with regard to the potential contributions you identified in Step 2. above?

4. Brainstorm within your group a list of measures the HR department could make to prove it is performing effectively in your assigned specialty area.

5. Within your group, identify HR's internal clients with regard to your assigned specialty area and draft a list of questions that HR should ask these internal clients in its self-evaluation quest.

6. Your instructor will ask each group to share its results. As each group presents, one member of the group will tape the group's flip chart paper to the chalkboard.

DEBRIEFING:

1. Why is it essential for an HR department to prove it adds value to the organization?

2. How can the HR department enhance its credibility within the organization?

3. Other than asking for feedback from its internal clients, how can HR track its performance in the specialty areas discussed during this exercise?

4. Do all organizations have the same expectations of HR?

5.   How will the expectations of HR in the 2000s be different from the expectations of the old "personnel" department?

6. SECOND-GUESSING THE HR PROFESSIONALS: DISCOVERING WHAT A FOCUS GROUP OF HR PROFESSIONALS SAID ABOUT NEEDED SKILLS AND COMPETENCIES OF NEW HR GRADUATES

 LEARNING OBJECTIVES:

1. To give you an opportunity to eavesdrop on the results of a focus group held with HR professionals in Toronto.

2. To learn what expectations HR professionals have of new HR graduates for the 21st century.

3. To discover what HR professionals have had to learn on their own after years in the field.

TYPE OF EXERCISE:

Small group activities and class-wide discussion

RELATED CONCEPTS:

*   HR development
*   Career development
*   Recruitment and selection
*   HR strategy

 TIME: 60 minutes

The initial class-wide review and recording of the students' answers to the questions will typically require 25 minutes. The small group discussion of the HR professionals answers and report to the class will take 20 minutes. The class-wide debriefing will require an additional 15 minutes.

BACKGROUND:

Today's HR graduates are painfully aware of the competitive world they are about to enter. One of the best preparations for the world of work in the HR field is to ask questions of those who are experienced in the HR field. HR professionals know all about the value and effectiveness of mentoring.

This exercise will give you the opportunity to second-guess how HR professionals in Toronto would answer a set of questions about their expectations for skill/competencies sets of new HR graduates and to learn about their perception of the effectiveness of their educational preparation for their career in HR.

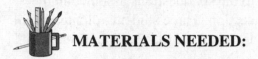 **MATERIALS NEEDED:**

- One copy of the ANSWERS FROM THE HR PROFESSIONALS' FOCUS GROUP sheet for each member of the class (as distributed by your instructor)

PREASSIGNMENT STUDENT PREPARATION:

Before the class in which you will completing this exercise, consider each of the following questions that were asked of a small group of HR professionals from a cross-section of corporations in Toronto during the course of a focus group session. Second-guess how the HR professionals answered these questions by writing down what you think they said during the focus group. The questions are:

1. What types of HR activities/roles would you expect a new HR graduate to be capable of performing upon joining a company?

2. In your experience, what are the key competencies and/or skills that HR students should have upon graduation in order to be effective and productive in HR roles?

3. Would you please identify any HR related skill, knowledge, behaviour that a recent new hire, intern or co-op student, was lacking? In what way did the student's educational institutional fail the student?

4. How would you select a new HR grad? What skills and/or competencies would you be looking for?

5. Think about your own experiences in HR related course work. What in your opinion was not taught that you later had to learn on your own or from an another HR professional?

6.   What do you see as key skills and/or competencies that new graduates in all fields should have to be top performers in the business world? Are these different from those you stated for the HR graduate in Question 2. above?

Please bring your answers to these questions to class.

PROCESS/INSTRUCTIONS:

1.   Your instructor will ask you to share your answers to the six questions assigned in the PREASSIGNMENT STUDENT PREPARATION section. Three student volunteers will be chosen to capture the essence of the answers on the chalkboard. The volunteers will record the answers to two questions each.

2.   Your instructor will distribute a copy of the material entitled: ANSWERS FROM THE HR PROFESSIONALS' FOCUS GROUP sheet to each member of the class. Take a few minutes to review the answers given by the HR professionals during the focus group.

3.   Your instructor will divide the class into small groups. Compare the differences and similarities between the aggregated class answers on the chalkboard and the answers given by the HR professionals. How do you explain the most notable differences?

4.   Your instructor will ask each group to report the essence of its discussion on any one notable difference between the class answers and those of the HR professionals.

DEBRIEFING:

1.   What did you learn about the expectations for entry roles and skills/competencies of new HR graduates?

2. What skills/competencies will a new HR graduate need to learn on his/her own? How will such skills/competencies be learned?

3. What recruitment and selection tips did you pick up from this exercise?

4. When you consider the HR professionals answers to Question 5. from the PREASSIGNMENT STUDENT PREPARATION section, how would you rate your own preparation for the HR field?

5. What skills/competencies should all new graduates entering the workforce in the early part of the 21st century have regardless of their field?

6.   What was the most surprising answer given by the HR professionals in the focus group
      session?

7. THE HR TREASURE HUNT:
DISCOVERING A MYRIAD OF RESOURCES FOR THE HR PROFESSIONAL

 LEARNING OBJECTIVES:

1. To heighten your awareness of the vast number and variety of resources available to the HR professional.

2. To assist you in making a faster transition from school to the world of the HR professional.

3. To augment your knowledge of HR terminology and the vast network of HR professionals.

4. To identify potential resources to assist you in your research in this and other HR courses.

TYPE OF EXERCISE:

Individual Internet research, small group activities, class-wide discussion

RELATED CONCEPTS:

*   Resources for HR professionals

 TIME: 35 minutes

The compiler groups will need 5 minutes to prepare for the class presentation. These groups will require 20 minutes total to give their reports. The web master group will be given 10 minutes to report.

BACKGROUND:

Two of the many important competencies for the HR professional for the 21st century are a zest for lifelong learning and continuous professional development. With the advent of new technologies, the HR professional is often only a "click" away from the vast array of invaluable resources now available around the world.

This exercise will lead you on a global treasure hunt in search of resources that will help you in this course and other HR courses, in your transition to the world of HR, and in your HR career.

PREASSIGNMENT STUDENT PREPARATION:

1. Your instructor will assign you to either the one "web master" group or to one of four "compiler" groups before the class in which you will be completing this exercise. The web master group's work begins after the work of the compiler groups have finished their research. The web master group will be designing web pages to showcase all the HR resource "treasures" the compiler groups find.

2. The four compiler groups will be each be assigned (by lottery) three specific HR topics to research and one general category called: "umbrella". The 12 specific topics available by lottery are: HR planning, employee relations and diversity, legal issues in HR, organizational development (including change management), organizational learning (including continuous learning and intellectual capital), recruitment and selection (including orientation), HR development (including career development), compensation and benefits (including rewards and recognition strategies), health and safety (including wellness), work/life balance, international HR, and employee communication (including employee newsletters, surveys and manuals). In addition to researching its three assigned specific topics, each compiler group will also be hunting for one-stop all-inclusive HR resource pools ("umbrella") i.e., Internet sites with links to a vast array of HR topics.

3. Each compiler group will be looking for the following types of resources for its umbrella list and specific topics lists and will organize the "treasures" it finds under these headings: Internet sites (including HR chat lines), your school library's HR materials, government offices, HR associations, HR consulting companies, HR magazines, HR books, and HR conferences. Each group will choose one icon to represent its specific lists and one for its umbrella list. Each group should make every effort to annotate its lists of resources. The final task of each compiler group will be to eliminate any duplication within its lists. The lists will be handed over to the web master group on disk. Be sure to include a list of group members' names and phone numbers.

4. The web master group will receive a disk containing the annotated lists from the four compiler groups. The first task of this group will be to collate the four umbrella lists, eliminate any duplication, and choose one icon to represent this list from the four different icons suggested by the compiler groups. Next, the web master group will design a web site that will showcase the amalgamated umbrella list and each of the specific topic lists. The web master group will then submit its web site material to your instructor.

PROCESS/INSTRUCTIONS:

1.   Each compiler group will be given 5 minutes to prepare a brief presentation on their reflections on their resource treasure hunt.

2.   Your instructor will ask each compiler group in turn to give a 5 minute report to the class.

3.   The web master group will give its reflections on the work of the compiler groups and will present the class with a copy of the web pages it has designed to showcase the umbrella and specific topic resources.

4.   During the course, you are encouraged to update your resource list and to share your changes with the class. Your instructor will ask you to submit information on new resources directly to him/her throughout the course.

FOLLOW-UP ACTIVITIES:

1.   The web master group should ask the instructor about posting their web design on the Internet under the name of the course.

2.   The class should send a copy of the final resources lists to the head of the your school's library.

PART 2

STRATEGIC HR MANAGEMENT

HR AND ORGANIZATIONAL TREND ANALYSIS

8. THERE'S NO BASE LIKE HOME:
LOOKING AT THE PERSONAL SIDE OF TELECOMMUTING

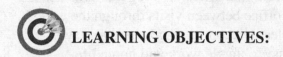 **LEARNING OBJECTIVES:**

1. To stimulate individual research on the Internet on telecommuting/telework.

2. To highlight the advantages and disadvantages of telecommuting for both the
    telecommuter worker and supervisor.

3. To explore strategies for increasing the success of telecommuting programs.

TYPE OF EXERCISE:

Individual activities and class-wide discussion

RELATED CONCEPTS:

*   Alternative work arrangements
*   Telecommuting
*   Work and home-life balance

 TIME: 40 minutes

The in-class time to share a summary of the students' submissions will typically require about
20 minutes. The reading of the second scenario and the debriefing will require another 20
minutes.

BACKGROUND:

Traditionally, telecommuting has been initiated by employees with the main reason being to improve employee lifestyle. There is evidence of an increasing interest in telecommuting as a management practice.

A survey by consulting firm KPMG reported that of the 20% of the 2025 Canadian organizations who responded to their survey, 4.5% had telecommuters on staff and another 26% used telecommuters occasionally. This survey predicted that "the greatest increases [in telecommuting] are expected in professional, technical and middle management roles." In this survey, 91% of employers required that telecommuters be in the office on a regular or as needed basis and that the telecommuters stay in touch with the office between visits through the use of teleconferencing, e-mail and written documents.[1] It is clear telecommuting is here to stay. However, while it has its advantages, it is not always easy to juggle work and home life, especially when they are physically blended.

This exercise will help you to examine the advantages and challenges involved in telework.

 MATERIALS NEEDED:

- Two sheets of unlined legal-sized paper
- One sheet of lined letter-sized paper
- One sheet of unlined letter-sized paper

PREASSIGNMENT STUDENT PREPARATION:

1. Go to the Internet to research the telecommuting (also known as telework). The InnoVisions Canada's site at http://www.ivc.ca/ is an excellent place to start. On a sheet of lined letter-sized paper, make a list of all the sites you visit and note in point form three or four key features of each site. Print your name on the top of your website list.

2. Read the following scenario:

   You are Aziz, a married twenty-nine year old father of two. Your wife, Erin, is a flight attendant with a Canadian airline company. You have a two year old son who attends play school three mornings week and a five year old daughter who is enrolled in full-day kindergarten. As a result of a motorcycle accident in your late teens, you have been confined to a wheelchair. Six months ago, your company, a non-unionized call centre with its headquarters located in the centre of large Canadian city offered you and your fellow call handlers the opportunity to participate in a year long telecommuting pilot program. Your supervisor explained that, while she was not altogether convinced that telecommuting was all it has been touted to be, she would allow her direct reports to take part in the pilot program. Further, she cautioned that they needed to be aware that the already stringent quotas would be increased and that she would be keeping very close tabs on their output.

3. Fold a sheet of unlined letter-sized paper in half from top to bottom. Turn the paper in "landscape" fashion. Entitle the left side "Aziz" and the right side "Supervisor". Answer the following questions in point form on a piece of paper. On the left side write your answer to the following question: Why do you think Aziz opted to participate in the telecommuting program in the first place? On the right side, answer the question: Why do you think his supervisor was so hesitant about the program at the beginning? Be sure to print your name on the top right of this paper.

4. Fold a blank sheet of unlined legal-sized paper into three sections from top to bottom. Turn the paper sideways ("landscape" fashion) so that you have the three folds appearing from left to right. Write "Aziz - Six Months Into the Program" at the top of this sheet. On one third of the sheet, list all the advantages of telecommuting that Aziz would have realized from the program after the first six months. On the next third of the sheet, list all the disadvantages he would have noticed in this time. On the final third of the sheet, suggest strategies that could help Aziz to address the disadvantages. Be sure to include a list of all the human and material resources you would need to implement. Print your name on the top right of this sheet.

5. Take a fresh sheet of unlined legal-sized paper. This time write "Supervisor - Six Months Into the Program" on the top of the sheet. Repeat Step 3. above but this time take the point of view of the supervisor.

6. Hand in all four sheets to your instructor within the specified time frame. Be sure you have printed your name of each sheet.

PROCESS/INSTRUCTIONS:

1. In class, your instructor will display a summary of the websites and answers generated in Steps 1., 2., 3. and 4. of the PREASSIGNMENT STUDENT PREPARATION section.

2. Read the follow-up scenario that will be distributed by your instructor.

DEBRIEFING:

1. What are the current statistics on telework in Canada? How do you expect these statistics to change in the next five years?

2. Which Canadian companies are using telework? At what levels are they using it?

3. What are the advantages of telework for individual telecommuters? For companies? For the communities in which these companies are located?

4. What are some of the possible disadvantages/challenges associated with telework for the individual teleworkers? For the supervisors?

5. How typical is the attitude of Aziz's supervisor? Why is she so skeptical about telecommuting? What training do supervisors require if their companies introduce telecommuting?

6. Discuss the conflicting feelings experienced by Aziz after six months.

7. What strategies and support mechanisms could be worked out between Aziz and his supervisor that would help him perform to the maximum in the telework program in the longer run?

FOLLOW-UP ACTIVITIES:

1. Obtain from your instructor a copy of the master list of telework websites displayed in class. Continue your research on the topic. Find out what the following terms mean: hoteling/free address and remote centres.

2. Contact one Canadian company which uses telework. Ask a company representative what type of personality best matches the challenges of telework.

3. Research other alternative work arrangements, such as: flexible hours, job sharing, sabbaticals, etc.

REFERENCE:

1.   Telecommuting Survey (1998); http://www.kpmg.ca/abc/vl/surveys/telcmut.htm

9. NET-WORKING:
FINDING A JOB ON THE INTERNET

 LEARNING OBJECTIVES:

1. To increase your awareness of the Internet as a recruitment tool for HR professionals and their organizations.

2. To give you an opportunity to explore the Internet as a recruitment resource and a job search aid.

TYPE OF EXERCISE:

Small group activities and class-wide discussion

RELATED CONCEPTS:

*   HR strategy
*   Recruitment and selection
*   Employee retention
*   Rewards and recognition
*   Organizational culture

 TIME: 40 minutes

The class-wide brainstorming sessions on the advantages and the disadvantages of the Internet recruitment process will typically require a total of 10 minutes. The small group session will take 20 minutes. The debriefing will require an additional 10 minutes.

BACKGROUND:

HR professionals are increasingly utilizing the Internet as a cost effective recruitment method and, as a result, the number of job postings are growing exponentially. This exercise will give you an opportunity to explore the Internet as a recruitment tool for HR professionals and a job search aid for job seekers.

PREASSIGNMENT STUDENT PREPARATION:

Before the class in which you will be completing this exercise, your instructor will ask you individually to explore a number of recruitment-oriented web sites. For each recruitment site, attempt to find the answers to the following questions:

- How is the site organized for job applicants?
- Is this an effective recruitment site? Why? Why not?
- Outline the process that an applicant would follow to submit an application in response to a job ad on this site?
- Is the process easy or difficult for the applicant to follow? Why? Why not?
- What recommendations could you offer for the improvement of the job application process?
- What can you learn of a company's organizational culture from the job ads? (Give three specific examples.)

PROCESS/INSTRUCTIONS:

1. As a class, brainstorm a list of the advantages of Internet recruitment advertising for HR professionals and their organizations. Next, brainstorm a list of the disadvantages?

2. Your instructor will divide the class into small groups. Share with your group what you learned about the Internet recruitment process by sharing your answers to the questions posed in the PREASSIGNMENT STUDENT PREPARATION section.

DEBRIEFING:

1. What are the advantages and disadvantages of utilizing an Internet recruitment process?

2.   Based on your individual Internet research and the discussions in your small group, what are the characteristics of an effective job posting site? Of an effective job posting?

3.   Based on your individual Internet research and the discussions in your small group, what are the characteristics of an ineffective job posting site? Of an ineffective job posting?

4.   How and why do companies reveal aspects of their organizational culture in the Internet recruitment process?

FOLLOW-UP ACTIVITIES:

1.   Design an optimal Internet application process for a clerical position at your school.

2.   Choose one job posting that you noticed during this exercise. Do further research on the company which advertised this opening. As you do more research on the company, seek to confirm your hypothesis about the type of organizational culture in the this company.

10. HR PROFESSIONALS WITH A GLOBAL REACH: A COMPETENCY MODEL FOR HR PROFESSIONALS WITH WORLDWIDE RESPONSIBILITIES

 LEARNING OBJECTIVES:

1. To facilitate your discovery and review of contemporary HR competency models.

2. To increase your awareness of the challenges which confront HR professionals in a global company.

3. To give you the opportunity to learn about the required competencies for HR professionals in a global company.

4. To give you information about the assimilation, training and development of HR professionals in a global company.

TYPE OF EXERCISE:

Individual Internet Research, small group activities and class-wide discussion

RELATED CONCEPTS:

*   Global HR
*   Competencies and skills
*   HR and organizational trend analysis
*   HR development
*   Globalization
*   Cultural differences
*   Cross-cultural training

 TIME: 60 minutes

Small groups will typically require 15 minutes for sharing the results of their Internet research with regard to the two assigned HR competency models and for choosing a third model. Five minutes will be needed to share the IBM HR information within the groups. The crafting of a fourth model is expected to take 15 minutes. The class presentations of the fourth model and rationale will take 15 minutes. The debriefing will require an additional 10 minutes.

BACKGROUND:

According to one human resources association [1], an HR competency model "is a vision of the proficiencies needed by the HR professional to compete and contribute successfully." Another HR association[2] says that "competency models have become a dramatic resource in refocusing people on what it takes to succeed in today's workplace."

This exercise will give you an opportunity to research and extend some HR Competency Models which are available to you on the Internet.

PREASSIGNMENT STUDENT PREPARATION:

1. Before the class in which you will completing this exercise, search the Internet for examples of HR Competency Models. To get you started, please visit the following two web sites and review the HR Competency Model and background material presented: http://www.linkageinc.com/ghri/competency.htm and http://www.nehra.org/meeting/prof/model.htm. Continue to search the Internet to find at least one other HR Competency Model. Study the HR Competency Models with a view to understanding what the state-of-the-art HR function in a global corporation might look like.

2. Further, before the class in which you will be completing this exercise, visit the web site of IBM (and IBM Canada linked to the IBM home site) at: http://www.ibm.com/. Explore the site with the view to understanding the HR function in this well-known global company. Be sure also to visit following IBM pages: http://www.empl.ibm.com/html/working_humanrcrs.html (a overview of the HR function); http://www.cybrblu.ibm.com/jobs/hr.html (a more extensive overview of the structure and operations of the HR function at IBM including socialization and professional development opportunities for HR new-hires); and http://www.cybrblu.ibm.com/jobs/cjobhr-1.html (an overview of full-time and co-op HR jobs at IBM). Please make notes on your visits to these sites and bring your notes to class.

 MATERIALS NEEDED:

- Four sheets of flip chart paper and one marker for each small group.
- One roll of masking tape.

PROCESS/INSTRUCTIONS:

1. Your instructor will divide the class into small groups. Within your group, share and discuss briefly the HR competency models you discovered as part of your Internet research in preparation for this class. Draw out a large-scale representation of the two HR competency models you were asked to find in the PREASSIGNMENT STUDENT PREPARATION section above on flip chart paper (one model on each of two sheets of paper).

2. Each person in your group will present the third model that he or she found on the Internet. Your group will choose the one best of these third models and will draw this model out on a third sheet of flip chart paper.

3. Share and discuss what you learned as a result of your Internet search about the HR function at IBM, a large well-known global company.

4. Your group will now take the role of the corporate HR team in a global company (such as IBM). You have been asked by the head of your unit, the VP, HR to craft an HR Competency Model using three such models (see Steps 1. And 2. above) as a point of departure for your task. Your unit has been asked to concentrate in particular on the globalized nature of your company. Within your small group, design an HR Competency Model that would be useful for your corporate HR professionals. Be sure to tape the three models side by side for inspiration on a wall or chalkboard near where your group is working. Draw this model out in large-scale on a fourth sheet of flip chart paper and make notes on your rationale for the model.

5. Your instructor will ask each group to present its HR Competency Model in turn.

DEBRIEFING:

1. What are the competencies necessary for an HR professional who is part of the corporate HR team in a large global company? Please give your rationale for including each competency.

2. What are the challenges which confront HR professionals who are part of the corporate HR team?

3. How does IBM assimilate, train and develop its newly hired HR professionals?

4. What should HR professionals in the corporate HR unit know about cultural differences? How will they acquire this knowledge?

REFERENCES:

1. The Northeast Human Resources Association;
http://www.nehra.org/meetings/prof/model.htm

2. The International Personnel Association; http://www.ipma-hr.org/training/pd.html

43

11. THIS IS WHAT WE STAND FOR: CRAFTING A SET OF CORE VALUE STATEMENTS

 LEARNING OBJECTIVES:

1.   To increase your awareness of the importance of a focus on ethical business practice.

2.   To give you experience in developing a set of core value statements..

TYPE OF EXERCISE:

Individual Internet research activities and small group

RELATED CONCEPTS:

- Core values
- Ethics
- Decision making

 TIME: 45 minutes

Small groups will typically require 20 minutes to craft a set of core value statements. The reading of the statements and voting will take 15 minutes. The debriefing will require an additional 10 minutes.

BACKGROUND:

A commitment to ethical practice is a core principle in business operations. Many businesses publish a values statement or credo or code of conduct. These are not simple lists of rules but, instead, they articulate the core values of the organization.[1] HR professionals and other key people in organizations insure that these principles are operationalized in the day-to-day operation of the business. It is, therefore, critical that HR professionals have a clear vision of the nature of the company's core values.

This exercise will give you experience in developing core value statements.

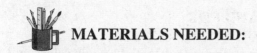 **MATERIALS NEEDED:**

- One sheet of flip chart paper
- One marker for each group
- One roll of masking tape

PREASSIGNMENT STUDENT PREPARATION:

Before the class in which you will be completing this exercise, visit the following web sites to review examples of core value statements and codes of ethics:

- Nortel Networks, Core Values: A Guide to Ethical Business Practices (http://www.nortel.com/cool/ethics/core.html);
- Johnson & Johnson, Our Credo (http://www.jnj.com/who_is_jnj/cr_usa.html);
- Texas Instruments, The Values and Ethics of TI (http://www.ti.com/corp/docs/ethics/brouchure/);
- The On-Line Journal of Ethics (http://condor.depaul.edu/ethics/ethg1.html);
- Centre for Applied Ethics: Publications and Individual Papers On-Line (http:www.ethics.ubc.ca/resources/business/pubs.html) and Canadian Centre for Ethics & Corporate Policy (http:www.ethicscentre.com/newslet.htm).

Make notes on these sites and bring your notes to class.

PROCESS/INSTRUCTIONS:

1. Your instructor will divide your class into small groups. Your group's task is to draft a set of core values statement for your business school. Use the statements you reviewed in the PREASSIGNEMENT STUDENT PREPARATION section as a guide. These core value statements would be used to introduce students, new staff and faculty to your business school's ethical foundation.

2. Write your group's core value statements on the flip chart paper provided by your instructor. When you have completed the exercise, post the sheet on the wall of your classroom.

3. When all the discussion groups have posted their statements, you will be given the opportunity to move around the classroom, read the statements and vote on the set of statements that you think best fit your business school. Your vote will be cast by putting an "X" in the upper right hand corner of the flip chart sheet containing the statements for which you wish to vote.

4. Your instructor will tally the votes and announce the winning core value statements.

DEBRIEFING:

1. If your business school were to adopt the core value statements selected by your class and commit to act on them, what aspects of the life of your business school would change (if any)? Please explain your answer.

2. Consider in what circumstances core value statements would be of help to students in your business school.

3. Who in your business school would be responsible for insuring the implementation of your core value statements?

FOLLOW-UP ACTIVITIES:

1. Invite your Dean or Chair to your class to review and comment on your core values statements and its applicability in your college or university.

2. Develop a code of conduct for students in your business school based on the core value statements that were developed by your class.

REFERENCE:

1. Core Values: A Guide to Ethical Business Practice;
    http://www/nortel.com/cool/ethics/core.html

HR STRATEGY DEVELOPMENT

12. FROM POLICY POLICE TO STRATEGIC PARTNER: LINKING HR MANAGEMENT SYSTEMS AND THE BUSINESS STRATEGY

 LEARNING OBJECTIVES:

1.   To give you a glimpse of the changing role of HR in contemporary organizations.

2.   To give you the opportunity to examine the linkage between the business strategy and the HR function.

3.   To demonstrate the importance of the linkage between the business strategy and the HR function.

4.   To have you identify the potential implications for HR systems as a result of HR planning.

TYPE OF EXERCISE:

Small group activities and in-class interview of a manager

RELATED CONCEPTS:

- HR strategy development
- HR and organizational trends analysis
- HR planning
- Business strategy
- Career development
- Evolution of HRM

TIME: 75 minutes (will be distributed over two different classes)

The sharing of the company data, drafting of the questions, the sharing of these questions class-wide and the choosing of the best questions will require a total of 30 minutes. The interview in class will take a maximum of 30 minutes. The debriefing will require about 15 minutes.

BACKGROUND:

In his book, *Human Resource Champions,* David Ulrich maintains that HR is at the crossroads of its existence.[1] While he has an ultimate and abiding faith in the value of the HR function as a key player in the competitiveness of the organization, he says that if HR does not add value and in fact, if it impedes performance in a company, it should be done away with i.e. outsourced. He urges HR professionals to change (and change now) from the mentality of "what we do" to "what we deliver" i.e., the outcomes, guarantees and results of HR work. "When HR practices are aligned with the needs of the internal and external customers, firms are more likely to succeed. They must move their HR professionals beyond the roles of policy police and regulatory watchdogs to become partners, players, and pioneers in delivering value."[2]

In his book, Ulrich advocates that in order to make this transition, HR professionals must assume four roles: strategic partner, administrative expert, employee champion, and change agent.

This exercise will give you the opportunity to explore the linkage between HR and the business strategy in contemporary organizations.

PREASSIGNMENT STUDENT PREPARATION:

Before the class in which you will be completing this exercise, your instructor will give you the name of a company to research.

PROCESS/INSTRUCTIONS:

1.   Your instructor will divide the class into small groups. Share with your group members the information you have gathered on the assigned company.

2.   In your group, draft a maximum of four questions you would like to ask senior line managers and HR managers in your assigned company. Your questions should focus on the following topics: key external and internal strategic issues facing this organization over the next two or three years, the organizational implications of these strategic issues e.g., changes in organizational structure and/or organizational processes, changes in the

types of roles required, changes in the total number of roles required, changes in career development patterns for individuals, etc. and the role that will be played by HR as a strategic partner.

3. Your instructor will ask each group to share its questions in round robin fashion with the class as a whole.

4. By consensus, decide on the best six to eight questions to ask management guests from your assigned company who will be invited to the next class by your instructor. Also agree on three or four different students who will act as interviewers. Your instructor will see that the guests receive a copy of the questions before the class.

5. In the next class, with your invited guests present, the interviewers will ask the agreed-upon questions. The debriefing for this exercise will take place after your management guests have left.

DEBRIEFING:

1. What is your assigned company's strategy for the next few years?

2. Will HR be playing the role of strategic partner over the next few years? Please explain your answer.

3.   What are the implications of the planned changes in your assigned company for the HR function?

4.   What should be the priorities for HR management in this company be over the next year? The following year? The year after that?

5.   What are the "deliverables" for the HR function in the next few years?

REFERENCES:

1.   Ulrich, D. (1996). *Human Resource Champions*. Boston, Mass.: Harvard Business School Press.

2.   Ibid., p. viii.

51

13. IN SEARCH OF COOL COMPANIES:
PROJECTING A CORPORATE IMAGE THROUGH NEWSPAPER ADS

 LEARNING OBJECTIVES:

1. To help you to appreciate the newspaper job ad as a vehicle for organizations to project an appealing corporate image to attract new talent.

2. To give you experience in critically assessing the corporate image an organization projects through its newspaper ads.

TYPE OF EXERCISE:

Small group activities and class-wide discussion

RELATED CONCEPTS:

- Recruitment and selection
- Corporate image

 TIME: 55 minutes

Small groups will typically require a maximum of 20 minutes to read the three ads supplied by each group member and to choose one of these ads for further analysis. The group then will require another 10 minutes to analyze the corporate image projected by their chosen organization. Finally, class presentations and debriefing will require an additional 15 minutes and 10 minutes respectively.

BACKGROUND:

One of the less obvious goals that Canadian organizations have for their substantial annual expenditures for newspaper job ads is to project a strong corporate image as a top employer within the community, across the country and even globally. For Canadian companies, such as those in the various segments of the computer industry, being able to project such a strong corporate image means having a competitive edge in attracting top talent in a tight job market.

This exercise will give you an opportunity to focus exclusively on the topic of corporate image as projected in the "Professional Help Wanted" columns. Further, you may want to extend this exercise with your own research into a particular organization's changing corporate image over time.

PREASSIGNMENT STUDENT PREPARATION:

Before the class in which you will be completing this exercise, look for newspaper job ads of three companies for which you might like to work. Bring copies of the ads to class.

 MATERIALS NEEDED:

- Three job ads supplied by each student in the class
- Two transparency sheets and one transparency marker per group

PROCESS / INSTRUCTIONS:

1. Your instructor will divide the class into small groups. Within your group, read each of the three ads that you and your classmates have brought to class. Each group member will explain why each of the three organizations is attractive as a potential employer.

2. Reach consensus within your group on the one organization for which you would all want to work. Discuss the strength and content of the corporate image that your chosen organization is projecting in the ad and why you would want to "buy in" to such an organization. Brainstorm what you think would be the characteristics of the candidate who would best fill the advertised job and who would fit in well in this particular company.

3. Assist your group in preparing a short presentation for the class in which you outline your chosen ad and summarize your group discussion from Step 2. above.

DEBRIEFING:

1. How do organizations use their newspaper job ads to project their corporate image?

2.   What were the similarities/differences in projected corporate image across the ads chosen by the groups?

3.   If you were to give an award for the overall "coolest" company (based on the corporate image projected in all the ads presented in the class reports), which company would win? Please explain your answer.

4.   If you were to give an award for the least "cool" company (based on the corporate image projected in all the ads presented in the class reports), which company would win? What recommendations do you have for this company?

FOLLOW-UP ACTIVITIES:

1.   Go to the web sites of the organizations which were discussed in the class reports. Do you find the corporate image projected throughout the web site to be consistent or inconsistent with the image projected in the ad? Please explain your answer.

2.   Look for a newspaper job ad in today's paper that advertises a job opening in one of Canada's banks. Analyze the corporate image projected in this ad. Do some research on the Internet on how the industry of your chosen organization has changed over the last two decades. Rewrite the ad to reflect the likely image projected in ads 20 years ago by this bank.

54

14. GOOD OLD CORPORATE U :
THE EMERGENCE OF CORPORATE UNIVERSITIES

 LEARNING OBJECTIVES:

1. To facilitate your review of the state-of-the-art of the ETS (education and training services) industry in Canada.

2. To understand the rationale for establishing a corporate university.

3. To understand the decision making processes corporations go through in establishing corporate universities.

4. To learn the criteria corporations use to measure the effectiveness of their corporate university.

5. To benchmark the practices of some established corporate universities.

TYPE OF EXERCISE:

Individual Internet research, small group activities, debate and class-wide discussion

 TIME: 60 minutes

The five groups will typically require 10 minutes for sharing the results of their Internet research. The preparation for the debate by the different groups will take 20 minutes. The reading of the rules established by the J Group will take 5 minutes. The debate will take a maximum of 15 minutes. The debriefing will require 10 minutes and will be followed by the adjudication results and rationale (5 minutes).

BACKGROUND:

The numbers of corporate universities have quadrupled in the last decade from 400 in 1988 to more than 1600 in 1999, including 40 percent of the *Fortune* 500 companies.[1] This exercise will give you an opportunity to understand this growing phenomenon.

PREASSIGNMENT STUDENT PREPARATION:

Before the class in which you will be completing this exercise you are asked to search the Internet for the answers to the following questions about corporate universities:

1. What is the state-of-the-art in the ETS (education and training) industry at present in Canada i.e., "characteristics", "trends and issues" and "the bottom line"? (http://www.strategies.gc.ca/SSG/bp0151e.html).

2. What is a "corporate university"? (http:www.kwheeler.com/Whatcu.htm; http://www.workinfo.com/wptfree/HRDdirectory/cuprop.html)

3. Why do corporations set up their corporate universities? (http://www.workinfo.com/wptfree/HRDdirectory/cuprop.html)

4. How should a company go about establishing a corporate university? (http://www.kwheeler.com/Cupresentation.htm; This is a Powerpoint presentation)

5. How do corporations measure the effectiveness of their corporate universities? (Http://www.corpu.com.news/specialinterest.htm)

6. Are corporate universities only for large corporations (as opposed for small to medium-sized)? (http://www.inc.com/incmagazine/archives/02990951.html)

7. What does a corporate university "look like"? (Motorola: http://www.kwheeler.com/Culist.htm; also search the archives for Motorola University on page 2 of the following site: http://www.traininguniversity.com/magazine/current/ Sears: http://www.sears.com/company/hr/suniv.htm; Volvo: http://www.traininguniversity.com/magazine/jan_feb98/volvo.htm; Disney: http://www.traininguniversity/may_jun96/disney2.orig.html; Dana: http://www.traininguniversity.com/magazine/mar_apr97/dana_facilities.html; see a list of corporate university list at: http://www.kwheeler.com/Culist.htm; also search for articles on corporate universities of interest for you in the archives of the *Corporate University Review* magazine (see page 2 of this address for the CUR archives button)from: http://www.traininguniversity.com/magazine/current)

PROCESS/INSTRUCTIONS:

1. Your instructor will divide the class into five equal groups. Within your group, share your answers to the questions posed in the PREASSIGNMENT STUDENT PREPARATION section above.

2. Your instructor will reorganize the groups in preparation for a class debate on the topic of "The Corporate University Boom: Business School Threat or Opportunity". One group will become the panel of judges (J Group) who will moderate the 15 minute debate and ultimately declare a winning side. Two groups will take the stance that corporate universities are a threat to business schools (T groups). The remaining two groups will take the stance that corporate universities represent a significant opportunity for business schools (O Groups).

3. Each of the T Groups and each of the O Groups will brainstorm for 10 minutes the key points they will want to bring out to score their points during the upcoming debate. For the next 10 minutes the two T Groups will join together to amalgamate their points into one final list. The O Groups will do the same. Each expanded group will choose one student to represent its side in the debate. During the 20 minute period set aside for this step, the J Group will draw up a set of rules and guidelines for the debate.

4. The J group will read its rules for the debate and then moderate the 15 minute debate. The J Group will be excused from the room during the DEBRIEFING section in order to discuss the debate and choose a winner (plus rationale). The J Group will announce its verdict after the DEBRIEFING session.

DEBRIEFING:

1. Why have corporate universities grown so much in the last decade? Will this trend continue?

2.   How do you see corporate universities in relation to the Business Schools - a threat or an opportunity? Please explain your answer.

3.   Contrast the key competencies or skills that would be required of a Dean of corporate university as compared with the Dean of your business school.

4.   Would you consider applying for the job of Chief Learning Officer in a large corporation or would you rather be an instructor in a business school? Please explain your answer.

FOLLOW-UP ACTIVITIES:

1.   Invite the Dean of your business school to class to express his or her side of the Threat or Opportunity debate and his or her view of the competencies required for his or her job as opposed to that of the Dean of a corporate university.

2.   Draw up a list of further resources on the topic of corporate universities.

REFERENCE:

1.   Executive Summary: 1999 Survey of Corporate University Future Directions; http://www.corpu.com/newsletter/survey.htm

15. FREE US UP TO DO OUR REAL JOB: EXPLORING OUTSOURCING AS A STRATEGY FOR HR

 **LEARNING OBJECTIVES:**

1.   To explore outsourcing as a strategy for the HR function in an organization.

2.   To give you an opportunity to delve deeper into the "Whys" of outsourcing.

TYPE OF EXERCISE:

Small group activities and class-wide discussion

RELATED CONCEPTS:

- HR strategy
- Outsourcing
- Change management

 TIME: 50 minutes

Small groups will typically require 20 minutes to consider the outsourcing possibilities, to discuss the pros and cons of their outsourcing plans and to share their findings with the class. The formulation of the change management plan, the sharing with the class and the debriefing will require an additional 10 minutes each.

BACKGROUND:

HR managers, as all other managers in contemporary Canadian organizations, are assessing their core competencies and seeking cost effective outsourcing alternatives to in-house resources. The Outsourcing Institute (http://www.outsourcing.com/home.htm) suggests the following, among others, as reasons for organizations to consider outsourcing i.e., to: 1. Reduce and control operating costs, 2. Improve company focus, 3. Gain access to world class capabilities, 4. Free internal resources for other purposes, 5. Gain access to resources not available internally, 6. Accelerate reengineering benefits, and 7. Provide solution for a function which is difficult to manage or is out of control. For HR, reason 4. above is especially germane i.e., free internal resources for other purposes. As the role of the HR professional changes and strategic tasks become the focal point, the HR function will need to consider outsourcing those tasks which are routine and/or of lower priority.

This exercise will give you the opportunity to increase your understanding of outsourcing in the context of the HR function.

 **MATERIALS NEEDED:**

- Two sheets of flip chart paper and a marker for each small group
- One roll of masking tape

PREASSIGNMENT STUDENT PREPARATION:

Before the class in which you will be completing this exercise, your instructor will ask you to explore the following web sites: the Outsourcing Institute (http://www.outsourcing.com/home.htm), KPMG (http://www.kpmg.ca/home.htm), Deloitte Touche Tohmatsu (deloitte.ca/) and Andersen Consulting (http://www.andersen.com/index.html). The Outsourcing Institute will increase your background knowledge of outsourcing. The other three sites will serve as background for the scenario you will be considering during exercise. Be sure to explore each site for the following topics: mission statement and services offered (especially management consulting services offered). Make notes on the sites and bring these with you to class.

PROCESS/INSTRUCTIONS:

1.   Please read the following scenario:

You are vice-president, HR for a large national consulting company. Your team of HR professionals support 15 000 employees across Canada. Your mandate for the next three years is to support the senior team of VPs in your company in the diversification of the consulting business from a focus on tax and accounting to a full service consulting company. The organizational goal is to work closely with the current complement of 10 000 consultants in order to move them from a specialist focus to that of a generalist. In addition, you are trying to attract new consultants to your company who have experience in reengineering, HR, and executive search. Currently your HR departmental team is comprised of 50 head office staff.

After significant analysis, you have determined that 80% of your department's time is being spent on the following administrative functions: benefits administration, clerical and administrative recruiting, compensation administration, and communication (company newsletter production). You know that you must reorganize and move your team to a new focus to fulfill your mandate. You are well aware that you cannot hire more staff. You have just recently become aware of outsourcing.

2.   Your instructor will divide the class into small groups. Share what you learned in your Internet search of the sites listed in the PREASSIGNMENT STUDENT PREPARATION section. In your small group, brainstorm the possibilities for outsourcing with respect to each administrative function listed near the end of the scenario. Be sure to assess the pros and cons of the outsourcing possibilities you mention. Record the essence of your group's discussion on the flip chart paper.

3.   Your instructor will ask each group to make a brief presentation on its deliberations.

4.   As a class, decide on the optimal outsourcing plan for this HR department.

5.   In your small group, decide on your plan of attack for fulfilling your new mandate i.e., to support the senior VPs in the diversification of the consulting business, the transition of the consultants from specialists to generalists, and the attracting of new consultants. Record the essence of your group's plan on the flip chart paper.

6.   Your instructor will ask each group to present its change management plan to the class.

DEBRIEFING:

1.   What are some of the concerns managers might have in general with outsourcing?

2.   Are there any concerns or risks specific to the HR function with regard to outsourcing? Please explain your answer.

3. What can the VP, HR do to address the outsourcing concerns you mention in your answer to Question 2. above?

4. What were the elements of the best change management plans suggested in class?

FOLLOW-UP ACTIVITIES:

1. In small groups, consider how the new mandate might be reflected on the company's organizational chart.

2. Conduct a telephone survey in your community to assess the current level of outsourcing (not restricted to the HR function) and to learn what areas are being outsourced?

REFERENCE:

1. Facts and Figures - The Outsourcing Institute's Annual Survey of Outsourcing End Users; http://www.outsourcing.com/howandwhy/surveyresults/index.htm

16. I NEED A STUDENT TO... :
IDENTIFYING FUNDING SOURCES AVAILABLE FROM THE CANADIAN GOVERNMENT TO HIRE A STUDENT

 LEARNING OBJECTIVES:

1.   To learn how to research government resources that are available to assist companies in funding summer and youth programs.

2.   To practice matching government programs with company needs.

3.   To advise a line manager about the most appropriate government program for which to apply and about the costs and benefits of that particular program for the company.

4.   To draft an outline of a proposal for funding to the sponsoring government agency.

TYPE OF EXERCISE:

Small group activities and class-wide discussion

RELATED CONCEPTS:

- Recruitment and selection
- HR and organizational trends analysis
- HR planning
- HR strategy development
- Person-job fit

 TIME: 55 minutes

Small groups will typically require 15 minutes to familiarize themselves with available government funding programs, to separate out those funding programs for which the company would qualify, and to decide on what documentation each application requires. The drafting of the letter to Shelley recommending a particular program and the proposal for the government agency sponsoring the program will each require an additional 15 minutes. Debriefing will require an additional 10 minutes.

BACKGROUND:

Hiring students for summer and/or part-time work can be a valuable win/win situation for the both students and employers. Canadian companies are usually eager to access government programs to offset the costs of hiring and paying students. HR professionals in organizations can provide a valuable link between government initiatives and line managers to insure that summer and youth programs are used to best advantage.

This exercise will raise your awareness of government resources and give you practice in the role of an HR generalist.

 MATERIALS NEEDED:

- Three sheets of flip chart paper and one marker per group
- One roll of masking tape

PREASSIGNMENT STUDENT PREPARATION:

Before the class in which you will be completing this exercise, your instructor will ask 6 or 8 students ("researchers") either to make a telephone call to the nearest office of HRDC (Human Resources Development of Canada) or to the constituency office of their federal or provincial member of parliament/legislature/national assembly or to visit the HRDC web site in search of details (criteria for qualifying, application forms, etc.) concerning current government-funded summer and youth programs. One researcher will be assigned to each small group and all materials gathered will be shared across all the small groups as background for this exercise.

PROCESS/INSTRUCTIONS:

1.   Your instructor will divide the class into small groups. Please read the following scenario:

> *You are the Human Resource generalist in a small company of 75 employees. Your company is in the business of developing creative marketing materials for a variety of different kinds of organizations. It has taken three years to get the business established. During its fourth and fifth years of operation, the company has doubled the volume of its business. Growth is projected to be very strong in the coming two years.*

Shelley is your company's Business Development Director. She has a small staff of two full-time managers each of whom is responsible for two business areas. Because of the increased volume, she has identified a need to hire a part-time student for an average of ten hours per week. This person would be responsible for updating client databases, researching client industries, and preparing client presentations. Shelley has come to you to talk about her plan and to find out what kind of government assistance is available to offset the cost of hiring a student.

2.   Under the direction of your researcher (see the section above entitled: PREASSIGNMENT STUDENT PREPARATION), familiarize yourself with the details of the various government funding programs available.

3.   In your role as an HR generalist for the small company (described in the scenario), determine for which programs your company qualifies, what documentation would need to be completed for each and what further information you would need to make a decision on which program to recommend to Shelley. Make notes on the flip chart paper supplied by your instructor.

4.   Write a memo to Shelley recommending the most appropriate program. In the memo, highlight the anticipated benefits (and costs) to your company if it ultimately receives the funding. Record the benefits and costs on a piece of flip chart paper.

5.   Develop a brief outline of the proposal which will accompany the completed application form that your company would submit to the government agency that sponsors the student hiring program. Record the headings and subheadings for your memo on a piece of flip chart paper.

•   Tape your completed flip chart paper on a wall in your classroom as directed by your instructor.

DEBRIEFING:

1.   What are some of the challenges involved in accessing government funding programs?

2.	With the kind of business and the historic and projected growth of this company in mind, describe the ideal student to fill this position (assuming the company gets the funding).

3.	Would another type of work arrangement (e.g., co-op) be more appropriate for this business at this time in its history? Explain.

17. WHO'S OUT THERE?:
UTILIZING CREATIVE SOURCING STRATEGIES TO PLAN

 LEARNING OBJECTIVES:

1.   To provide opportunities for you to do some creative problem solving on how to attract key talent for an organization faced with a competitive market for new talent.

2.   To help you to benchmark those Canadian companies who excel at sourcing and attracting key talent.

TYPE OF EXERCISE:

Small group activities and Internet searches

RELATED CONCEPTS:

*   HR strategy development
*   Recruitment and selection

 TIME: 65 minutes

Small groups will typically require 15 minutes to review the Classified ads and to list and rank-order the three professional positions. The instructor and the runners will require 5 minutes to finalize the positions to be assigned to each group. The simultaneous activities of searching the Internet and the brainstorming of the sourcing strategies will require 20 minutes. Finally, the preparation and the delivery of the class reports and the debriefing will take a total of 25 minutes.

BACKGROUND:

In some areas of the economy, there is a critical shortage of appropriately trained personnel. Such a situation makes recruitment a major challenge for companies striving to compete. Traditional sourcing strategies such as placing ads in the newspapers may no longer be the most effective for attracting top talent in a highly competitive recruiting environment. In these circumstances, HR professionals are called upon to find creative solutions to the "talent wars".

This exercise will challenge you to develop creative sourcing strategies and will help you to become more aware of the variety of creative strategies that some Canadian companies are currently using to attract much-needed new talent.

 MATERIALS NEEDED:

- A minimum of 4 Classified Sections from current newspapers (preferably 2 national and 2 local for each group)
- One computer (with Internet access) and printer
- One overhead transparency and transparency marker per group

PREASSIGNMENT STUDENT PREPARATION:

Your instructor will ask you to bring to class copies of the Classified Sections from a variety of national and local newspapers.

PROCESS/INSTRUCTIONS:

1. Your instructor will divide the class into small groups. Each group will review the "Professional Help Wanted" ads in the Classified Sections of 4 different newspapers (2 national and 2 local). Each group will then select any three professional positions which appear to be in high demand. Each group will rank order the three positions in accordance with the amount of interest group members have in researching the particular position for the purposes of this exercise. (Note: #1 is the position most members of the group would like to research and #3 is the position they would least prefer to research.) The group will the elect one person for the position of "runner". The runners will take their group's list of three rank-ordered positions and meet briefly together with the instructor to make a final selection on the positions the groups will research (i.e., a different position for each group). Runners will make ever effort to represent the preferences of their group. The runners will report back to their group on their assigned position.

2. In each group, brainstorm a list of Canadian companies (local and national) which would be likely to be looking to fill such a position. Assign two students ("web searchers" in your group to locate and search the web sites of as many of these companies as possible in the time available. Web searchers will scour each web site looking for any information posted on recruitment strategies. At same time as these two students are searching the Internet, the remaining group members will brainstorm as many potential sourcing strategies (excluding newspaper ads) as they can for their assigned position. For each sourcing strategy, explain why you think it would be a successful strategy for the professional context on which you are focusing.

3. Each group will prepare a short report (one transparency maximum) for the class. Elect a spokesperson for the group ("reporter"). Be sure to print the name of the professional position you researched across the top and then list a few Canadian companies which routinely search for such a position. Finally, list on the transparency your creative sourcing strategies in bullet form.

4. Your instructor will ask each reporter in turn to present the findings of her/his group.

DEBRIEFING:

1. Which of the sourcing strategies presented in class were the most creative?

2. Which of the sourcing strategies presented in class were the most creative and likely to be the most effective?

3. Would you recommend the use of the Internet as a sourcing strategy? Please explain your answer.

4.   What advice would you have for a Canadian high tech company wanting to use the Internet to attract top talent who happen to belong to the same generation as you do?

FOLLOW-UP ACTIVITIES:

1.   Draft a letter to the HR Department for one Canadian company studied during this exercise in which you share some of the most appropriate and creative strategies mentioned in class.

2.   Design a web page for any one of the companies identified during this exercise for the sole purpose of attracting much-needed new talent.

3.   Obtain a list of web addresses for a number of well-known "headhunter" companies. Search their sites for additional sourcing strategies.

EMPLOYEE RELATIONS AND DIVERSITY

18. GUESS HOW MUCH WE MISSED YOU LAST WEEK: IDENTIFYING THE COSTS OF ABSENTEEISM AND RECOMMENDING STRATEGIES TO REDUCE COSTS

 LEARNING OBJECTIVES:

1.   To raise your awareness of the costs of absenteeism.

2.   To give you the opportunity to identify both the hard and soft costs of absenteeism.

3.   To give you some hands-on experience in recommending strategies for attendance management.

TYPE OF EXERCISE:

Individual activities, small group activities and class-wide discussion

 TIME: 40 minutes

The class as a whole will require 10 minutes to share their research on absenteeism/attendance management. Small groups will require 15 minutes to analyze and make their recommendations for Shams. The debriefing is expected to take another 15 minutes.

BACKGROUND:

The skyrocketing costs of absenteeism in work organizations across Canada is a matter of great urgency for management. Like voluntary turnover, absenteeism is a form of employee withdrawal. Absenteeism has been linked in the research literature with both low job satisfaction and low organizational commitment[1] but the strength of these relationships have been found to be modest. This suggests that there are many and various other reasons for absenteeism from work. HR can build business cases that highlight improved management practices as a way to reduce absenteeism and to increase job satisfaction.

 **MATERIALS NEEDED:**

- Three sheets of flip chart paper and one marker for each small group
- One calculator for each small group
- One roll of masking tape

PREASSIGNMENT STUDENT PREPARATION:

In preparation for the class in which you will be discussing this exercise, do some Internet research on the topic of absenteeism/attendance management. In particular, attempt to answer the following questions:

- What are the estimated annual costs of absenteeism for work organizations in Canada? In the United States?
- What are the reasons for absenteeism in Canadian work organizations?
- What strategies have been proposed in the management literature for attendance management i.e., to reduce absenteeism?

Your instructor will suggest some web sites to get you started. Bring a summary of your findings and a list of web sites and research sources to class.

PROCESS/INSTRUCTIONS:

1. Your instructor will ask you to share your Internet research findings with the class as a whole by asking each of the questions assigned in the PREASSIGNMENT STUDENT PREPARATION section. Three student volunteers will be chosen to capture the main ideas from the research on the chalkboard i.e., one student will note all cost-related information, another will note the reasons for absenteeism and the third will note strategies for reducing absenteeism.

2. Your instructor will divide the class into small groups. Please read the following scenario:

   Shams graduated two years ago from a Canadian post-secondary institution. His major was business administration. For personal reasons, he decided to take a job in his home town with a small non-unionized company (80 employees). This company which grows, sells and distributes potted plants is beginning to make quite a name for itself in Canada and has begun to export to the United States. Shams is one of the three telephone order takers in this company. He is becoming increasing bored with the work. In the last six months, Shams has been absent six Fridays. His supervisor, Mary Henhawk, is not a *pleased with his attendance record. The two other order takers are complaining about the extra work and stress that Shams' absences are causing for them. Mary is well aware that each order taker handles on average $10 000 in sales per day.*

3. In your group, calculate the dollar value of Shams' absences. Note your answer on the sheet of flip chart paper. Make a list of other costs associated with the absences of Shams. Again, note your list of associated costs on the same sheet of flip chart paper. On the another sheet of paper, brainstorm a list of possible reasons for Shams' absences. On a third sheet of paper, recommend strategies for his supervisor, Mary Henhawk to use with Shams.

4. Your instructor will ask the groups in turn to share their work on the costs, reasons for absences and attendance management strategies.

DEBRIEFING:

1. In your opinion, what was the single best attendance management strategy suggested for Shams? Please explain your answer.

2. What role should disciplinary action play in Shams' case?

3. What are the hard and soft costs associated with absenteeism in work organizations?

4.   What are the most effective strategies in general for attendance management?

5.   What training do supervisors need with regard to attendance management?

6.   How would attendance management strategies differ in a unionized company versus a non-unionized company like Shams'?

FOLLOW-UP ACTIVITIES:

1.   Simulate an initial fact-finding meeting between Mary Henhawk and Shams where Mary is genuinely interested in learning "what's up" with Shams and why he has been away so much on Fridays.

2.   Develop a disciplinary action plan for Mary Henhawk to use with Shams (in case she decides on this route). Next, alter the same plan for use in an unionized company which is otherwise similar to Shams'.

REFERENCE:

1.   Greenberg, J., Baron, R.A., Sales, C.A. and Owen, F.A. (2000). *Behaviour In Organizations.* Scarborough, Ont.: Prentice Hall Canada, pp. 175-176.

19. YOU'RE LUCKY I'M SO OBJECTIVE: SELECTION DECISIONS AND OBJECTIVITY

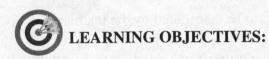 **LEARNING OBJECTIVES:**

1.   To give you an opportunity to examine the objectivity of selection decisions.

2.   To make you aware of "opportunities" for perceptual biases during the selection process.

TYPE OF EXERCISE:

Individual activity, small group activities and class-wide discussion

RELATED CONCEPTS:

- Recruitment and selection
- Perception
- Individual differences

 TIME: 40 minutes

The individual ranking activity will typically take 5 minutes. The first small group activity in which students reach a consensus ranking will require 15 minutes. Finally, the second group activity and debriefing will take 10 minutes each.

BACKGROUND:

Matching an individual applicant with the right job is a complex and, most often, subjective process. Selection is a core function for HR professionals. A lot rests on finding the right talent to add value to an organization and mistakes can be costly. Hiring mistakes can lead to wrongful dismissal lawsuits that can be expensive both financially and in terms of poor public relations both inside and outside of the organization. This puts considerable pressure on the HR professional who must insure that the match of person and job is as good as possible.

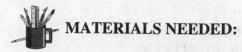 **MATERIALS NEEDED:**

- One applicant profile and one rating sheet for each student in the class (to be distributed by your instructor).
- One transparency marker and two rating sheets copied onto transparency sheets for each group
- One transparency marker and rating sheets copied onto transparency sheets for the student who tallies the votes
- One applicant profile for each student in the class (to be distributed by the instructor).

PROCESS/INSTRUCTIONS:

1.   Please read the following scenario:

   You are a Human Resource professional employed by a large marketing company in downtown Fredericton, New Brunswick. Your company is growing rapidly and is expanding globally. Your job is to select staff for a large number of entry level positions for the company's branch offices in Fredericton and the immediate surrounding area. You have finished all the interviews with the applicants for all positions and have now reached the final stage in the selection decision process. Today you are making the final decision on the applicants for the telemarketing positions. In fact, you have only one more applicant for whom you will make a final "accept/reject" decision before you leave for the day.

2.   Your instructor will ask for one volunteer from the class who will tally the rating sheets as soon as they are handed in at the end of this step. Next, your instructor will distribute a short applicant profile and a rating scale to each person in the class. Please do not discuss the applicant or rating scale with anyone else. As soon as you receive the profile, read it thoroughly, complete the rating scale and write your identification number (found on the top right of your copy of the profile). Your instructor will collect the completed rating scales. You will keep the applicant profile with you.

3.   Divide into small groups according to the FIRST number of your identification number i.e., all number 1s (11, 12, 13, 14, etc.) will form a group, all the 2s (21, 22, 23, 24, 25) will form a group and so on until all students are in a group. Your instructor will assist you by calling out one number at a time and indicating where your group will work.

4.   Your job is to reach a consensus (on all three questions on the rating sheet and the accept/reject final decision). When your group has reached a consensus, obtain from your instructor a transparency sheet which has a copy of the rating sheet printed on it. Mark the number of your group as your identification number on the top of the sheet i.e., a 1 or 2 or 3, etc. and then complete the sheet indicating the group's position on the applicant.

Hand the completed transparency sheet to the instructor.

5. Divide into a different small group. This time divide on the basis of your SECOND number of your identification number i.e., all the "1s" form a group (11, 21, 31, 41, 51, etc.), all the 2s form a group (12, 22, 32, 42, etc.) until all students are in a new group. Repeat Step 4. above. This time your group number will be the second number that you all have in common. The tally sheet will bear this number and the words "Mixed Group" written on the top.

6. The student who tallied the results of the first vote now share the results with the class. The instructor will share the rest of the results.

DEBRIEFING

1. Compare and contrast the individual votes with those of the groups.

2. Were the results of the second vote on the applicant rating sheet very different from your own individual ranking on your first rating sheet? How do you explain the results now?

3. What was the real purpose of this exercise? Did it succeed in its purpose?

20. CELEBRATING DIFFERENCES:
SHOWCASING DIVERSITY PROGRAMS IN CONTEMPORARY CANADIAN ORGANIZATIONS

 LEARNING OBJECTIVES:

1. To introduce you to a variety of diversity programs currently in use.

2. To increase your awareness of the importance to the HR professional of diversity promotion programs.

TYPE OF EXERCISE:

Group Internet research, small group activities and class-wide discussion

RELATED CONCEPTS:

*   Diversity
*   HR strategy

 TIME: 50 minutes

Small groups will require 20 minutes to develop a master list. Presentations to the class will take 20 minutes. Debriefing will require an additional 10 minutes.

BACKGROUND:

HR professionals have a major investment in the development and implementation of diversity programs in their organizations. The challenge of encouraging people of different genders, ages, cultures, races, nationalities and capabilities to work together to accomplish common organizational goals is a major part of the role of the HR professional. This exercise will give you the opportunity to learn about the diversity programs currently in use in various large organizations and to increase your awareness of issues related to diversity in contemporary organizations.

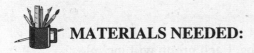 **MATERIALS NEEDED:**

- One sheet of flip chart paper and one marker for each small group
- One roll of masking tape

PREASSIGNMENT STUDENT PREPARATION:

1.   Before the class in which you will be completing this exercise, your instructor will divide the class into four task groups. Each group will be assigned one company or information site to research before the class in which diversity issues are to be discussed. The following is a list of sites that are good research starting points for each of the four task groups:

- Diversity at Texas Instruments: http://www.ti.com/corp/docs/diversity/background.htm
- Working at Kraft: http://kraft.neog.com/careers/work/put/diver.html
- EDS-Walking the Walk: http://www.eds.com/careers/working_at_eds/cr_walking_the_walk.shtml
- IBM Canada Valuing Diversity: http://www.can.ibm.com/headlines/cnib/index.htm and
- IBM Diversity: http:www.empl.ibm.com/diverse/workplace.index.html

2.   As a task group, visit the site you were assigned. Take note of the commitment that each company has made to diversity. Make a list of the strategies that each organization has developed to support this commitment. Each member of the task group will need a copy of this list to take to class.

3.   Visit the following sites to gather information on a wide range of issues related to the promotion of diversity:

- Diversity at Work: http://www.diversityatwork.com/twi/company.htm
- National Institute of Disability Management and Research: http://www.nidmar.ca/
- HR Diversity Links: http://www.shrm.org/hrlinks/div.htm

Based on your reading of these and related sites, make a list of additional strategies that an organization could undertake to support diversity. Each member of the group will need a copy of this list to take to class.

PROCESS/INSTRUCTIONS:

1.   Your instructor will divide the class into small groups. Each group will include representatives from each of the four task groups from the PREASSIGNMENT STUDENT PREPARATION section.

2.   Appoint one person to be the reporter for your discussion group. Within your group, review the lists made by each task group. Identify the similarities and the differences in the lists and develop a master list that identifies what your group believes are the most important aspects of a diversity program. Record your list on the flip chart paper provided by your instructor and post it on a wall of the classroom.

3.   Your instructor will ask each group's reporter in turn to describe the group's recommendations to the class.

DEBRIEFING:

1.   If you were a new employee in the organization that your task group studied, how do you think you would react to the diversity strategies described on the company's web site?

2.   Think about an organization with which you are familiar. Based on the work you have done in this exercise, what recommendations would you make to that organization concerning the development of their diversity programs?

FOLLOW-UP ACTIVITIES:

1. Interview an HR professional in your area concerning how she/he develops and implements diversity programs.

2. Visit an advocacy group that promotes the welfare of people who are in minority positions. This may include groups such as those dedicated to a particular cultural or racial group or organizations that focus on the needs of people who have physical, intellectual or emotional challenges. Interview their members about the kinds of measures they would like to see organizations undertake to secure their position.

LEGAL ISSUES IN HR

21. THAT'S THE LAST STRAW, YOU'RE OUT OF HERE TODAY!: UNDERSTANDING EMPLOYMENT LEGISLATION ON TERMINATION

 LEARNING OBJECTIVES:

1.   To sensitize you to the legal complexities surrounding employee discipline and termination in situations involving unauthorized employee absences.

2.   To inform you about appropriate management strategies for handling cases of unauthorized employee absences.

TYPE OF EXERCISE:

Individual Internet search, small group activities, and class-wide discussion

RELATED CONCEPTS:

- Legal Issues in HR
- Federal and provincial employment legislation
- Progressive discipline
- Absenteeism
- Termination/wrongful dismissal

 TIME: 50 minutes

The sharing of the Internet research and the outline of the conversation will typically take 10 minutes. Drafting the plan for Luke and presenting to the class will take 15 minutes each. The debriefing will require an additional 10 minutes.

BACKGROUND:

The following scenario is familiar to many HR professionals. The holidays are over and one employee fails to return to work. If this is clearly an isolated incident, a supervisor may be tempted to overlook the problem this time. However, consider the case of the chronic absentee, the person who is chronically a day or two late returning from vacations or who calls in with weak excuses for days off at other times of the year. While employers may be very upset by a single unauthorized employee absence taken at the company's busiest time of year, this in and of itself may not be sufficient to terminate that employee. The last thing the company wants is a wrongful dismissal suit.

One very important strategy in addressing the absenteeism issue is to insure that the organization has an absenteeism policy that specifies penalties for unauthorized/inappropriate absences. It is wise to include a statement "that says, 'An absence of three consecutive days without proper notification is job abandonment and is a voluntary termination.' "[1]

Further, it is good supervisory practice to review employee records on a regular basis to note and evaluate employee patterns of absenteeism. If an unusual rate of absenteeism and/or pattern of absences is evidenced in an employee's file, then the supervisor should begin to document the employee's absences with special care from that point in time. The supervisor should meet with the employee to discuss the employee's absenteeism. This meeting should be focused on problem solving rather than blame. If there is a reasonable explanation for the absences, the supervisor may be able to help find a solution to the underlying problem. For example, if the employee is experiencing difficulties with child care, the supervisor may be able to offer some alternative work arrangement such as flextime or, perhaps, job sharing. In any case, the essence of the conversation in the meeting should be documented and the record placed in the employee's file.

If the absenteeism persists, a clear distinction will need to be made between appropriate and inappropriate absenteeism. Since the negative fallout from chronic inappropriate absenteeism is felt throughout an organization over time, further decisive action by the supervisor will need to be taken - but only in accordance with federal and provincial employment legislation. The supervisor must now meet with the employee after the next inappropriate absence. After this meeting , the supervisor will write a letter of concern about this absence and will place it in the employee's file. If the absences persist, a second letter will be written by the supervisor specifying that continuation of the behaviour may result in termination. In the case of culpable absenteeism, disciplinary strategies such as suspension should also be considered. When all these efforts fail, termination may be considered but only after careful review of the circumstances to insure that every option has been exhausted.[2] A key issue for HR professionals is to insure that every avenue has been exhausted, that all labour legislation has been followed appropriately and that employees have been given every reasonable consideration before an action as drastic as termination is considered.

This exercise will give you an opportunity to outline an appropriate course of action for a supervisor to take when faced with an employee who is chronically absent.

 **MATERIALS NEEDED:**

• Two sheets of flip chart paper and one marker for each small group
• A roll of masking tape.

PREASSIGNMENT STUDENT PREPARATION:

Before the class in which you will complete this exercise, you should research federal and provincial employment standards on the Internet. Human Resources Development Canada's Human Resource Office for Employers web site (http://www.hroe.org/) is an excellent resource for learning about employment standards and practices all across Canada. When you visit this site, you will first choose which language you prefer. Next, you will choose a province. At this point, you will have arrived at the home page of your selected province. On this page, you should click on the button for "Layoffs and Termination". Next, you will be offered a number of useful buttons i.e., "Communications" (includes information on termination interviews and employee dismissals), "Legal Issues" (related to terminations e.g., wrongful dismissal) and "Employment Standards Issues For layoffs and Terminations" (termination is the focus of this exercise). Explore these areas and their links and make notes for class.

PROCESS/INSTRUCTIONS:

1. Your instructor will divide the class into four-person discussion groups. Briefly share the results of your Internet search of the Human Resource Office For Employers' web site.

2. Please read the following scenario:

   You are Carlo, a senior HR officer in the head office of a large office supplies chain. You have just come back from lunch and are reviewing your voice mail. The first message is from Luke, the supervisor from New Accounts Processing. He has left you a very distressing and urgent message. In a very angry tone of voice, he demands that you draw up termination papers immediately for Jaki, a clerk who has worked in his department since she joined the company three years ago. He says she was to return from her holidays today, Monday, but as of noon (it's now one hour later) she had not shown up for work and had not contacted him. He says he has had it with her absences and wants the termination papers to be sent by courier to Jaki's home by the end of the day.

3. Each group will take the role of Carlo, the HR officer. Write an outline of the conversation you will have immediately and in person with Luke, Jaki's supervisor. You are certain if you were to do as Luke asked, your company would find itself fighting a charge of wrongful dismissal. Your first task is to get Luke to calm down and understand the legal ramifications of his request. Record your outline (using words and/or phrases) on a sheet of flip chart paper.

4.   Your instructor will ask each group in turn to share its outline for the upcoming conversation with the class.

5.   Pretend that you have had the conversation with Luke and everything went as planned. You learned about Luke's frustration with Jaki's chronic absences, all of which Luke recalls have been on the heels of holidays. You also learned that Luke has never made any record of Jaki's absences and has never once talked to her about the problem. Luke has made an appointment tomorrow to meet you at 8:30 a.m. to make a plan on how to handle the situation with Jaki from this point. Continue in your role as Carlo and outline the steps that Luke should take in his plan of action. Record your key points on a sheet of flip chart paper.

6.   Your instructor will ask each group in turn to present its plan to the class.

DEBRIEFING:

1.   Discuss what would have happened if Carlo had done what Luke asked.

2.   Discuss Luke's motivation in requesting Jaki's swift dismissal. What could be some of the more "understandable" reasons for Jaki's absences? Name a work alternative that could be offered to Jaki in the event of each.

3.   Now that you have heard all of the plans made by the various groups for Luke, what is the best course of action for him to follow in the future with Jaki?

REFERENCES:

1.   Nip Absenteeism Before It Nips You, Smart Workplace Practices newsletter;
      http://www.smartbiz.com/sbs/arts/swp32.htm

2.   Guidelines for Absenteeism Control;
      http://benefits.org/interface/cost/absent2.htm#topofpage

22. SORRY, BUT YOUR SERVICES ARE NO LONGER REQUIRED: CHOOSING AN OUTPLACEMENT SERVICE PROVIDER TO SUPPORT DOWNSIZING

 LEARNING OBJECTIVES:

1.   To highlight the role outplacement can play to support downsizing in contemporary organizations.

2.   To investigate the various services offered by outplacement organizations.

3.   To provide you with the opportunity to compare and contrast a number of contemporary outplacement organizations.

TYPE OF EXERCISE:

Individual Internet research, small group activities and class-wide discussion

RELATED CONCEPTS:

*   HR planning
*   HR and organizational trend analysis
*   Downsizing
*   Termination of employment
*   Legal issues in HR

 TIME: 55 minutes

Sharing the yield from your Internet search with your group and reading the scenario will typically require 15 minutes. The assessment and final recommendation on your assigned outplacement organization will take 10 minutes. The class presentations will require 15 minutes. Finally, the vote and the debriefing will require an additional 15 minutes.

BACKGROUND:

The nasty 90s will long be remembered by many, including middle- and upper-level managers, as the era of downsizing and termination. Some organizations offer terminated employees an assistance program called "outplacement counselling" to help them to find alternate employment elsewhere. Many companies have chosen to outsource their outplacement services to outside specialists, such as: KPMG, Drake Beam Morin (DBM), Mainstream Access, Miller Dallas, Right Associates, RW Caldwell Associates Inc. and Morgan & Banks. The costs to employers of providing such outplacement services vary dramatically across outplacement organizations depending on the number of service elements provided to clients i.e., self-assessment and counselling, job search skills including résumé writing, work space, office equipment such as: computers, fax machine, photocopier, clerical assistance, mail services, information on the labour market and trend analysis.[1]

This exercise will give you the opportunity to learn about the role of outplacement in downsizing and termination and about the various service elements offered to clients by outsourced outplacement organizations.

 MATERIALS NEEDED:

- Seven 3" x 5" index cards for the outplacement organization lottery (supplied by your instructor)
- One sheet of flip chart paper and one marker for each of the seven small groups
- One roll of masking tape

PREASSIGMENT STUDENT PREPARATION:

1. Before the class in which you will be completing this exercise, visit the web sites of the following organizations who offer outplacement services:

   - Mainstream Access Corp. (http://www.mainstreamaccess.com/)
   - KPMG Canada (http://www.kpmg.ca/es/home.htm)
   - R.W. Caldwell Associates, Inc.(http://www.rwcaldwell.com/)
   - Right Associates (http://www.rsv.com/catalog.htm)
   - Miller Dallas Inc. (http://www.millerdallas.com/)
   - Morgan & Banks (http://www.morganbanks.com.au/index.htm)
   - Drake Beam Morin Canada (http://www.dbmcanada.com/)

   For each organization, please note the following information: location of the organization, range of outplacement/career transition services offered and client base (employee/management level). Please bring your notes to class.

2. Visit the web site of Human Resources Development Canada's Human Resource Office For Employers (http://www.hroe.org/t3.cfm?catnum=10&subcatnum=57&lang=EN&prov_code=ON). At this site, you will find links to two articles by William S. Frank, President of CareerLab entitled: 1. Costly Outplacement Mistakes Can Hinder Downsizing Efforts and 2. How Outplacement Prevents Lawsuits. Please read each article and make notes. Please bring your notes to class. (For your information, CareerLab's web site is http://www.careerlab.com).

PROCESS/INSTRUCTIONS:

1. Please read the following scenario:

    You are a Director, Employee Relations for a large hospital in Toronto. As a result of recent restructuring, you are eliminating 3 director-level positions. The average annual salary for a director-level position is $85 000. You have been asked by the Chief Operating Officer (COO) to investigate a number of large outplacement organizations. You are to review the services offered and to recommend an interim list of three providers for outplacement for these terminated persons. All three of these individuals are based in or around the Toronto area. All have between 8 to 15 years experience in hospital administration. Two of the three would be willing to relocate for other opportunities.

2. Your instructor will assign you to one of seven small groups. Within your group, share the information you gathered during your Internet search on the outplacement organizations and review the two articles written by William Frank of CareerLab as assigned in the PREASSIGNMENT STUDENT PREPARATION section above.

3. Your instructor will assign one of the seven outplacement organizations to each group by asking a volunteer from each group to participate in a lottery. For your organization, make a list of outplacement services that this particular organization could offer to your three terminated senior hospital administrators. Record the list on a sheet of flip chart paper. Consider what cost information you would want from the organization and the implications of the location of your outplacement organizations. Note this information on your sheet of flip chart paper. Make a decision as to whether or not you would recommend this organization as a potential provider for the three senior administrators (pending cost information, of course!) and note the final rationale offered by your group. Indicate your decision by writing either "Recommended" or "Not Recommended" on the bottom of the flip chart paper.

4. Your instructor will ask each group in turn to present its flip chart summary and rationale for the final decision for its particular outplacement organization. A representative of each group will tape its summary on the chalkboard at the front of the classroom.

5. Your instructor will ask you to vote for your top three choices of "best fit" outplacement organizations i.e., which of the three organizations you would want to continue to investigate before you write your report to your COO.

DEBRIEFING:

1. Why do companies hire outplacement organizations?

2. How could outplacement prevent lawsuits?

3. What some of the "outplacement mistakes" that have been made by companies in their haste to downsize?

4. What are the various types of services that outplacement organizations offer terminated employees? Upon what factors did you base your "top three outplacement organizations" decision?

5. Should you recommend the same outplacement service package and the same provider to all three of your terminated hospital adminstrators? Please explain your answer.

6. Should a company which is in a downsizing/restructuring mode provide outplacement services to all levels of staff? Please explain your answer.

FOLLOW-UP ACTIVITIES:

1. Contact local large organizations who have undergone restructuring in recent years and ask if they utilize(d) an outplacement organization for terminated staff or if they offer(ed) outplacement services to staff as an in-house program.

2. Choose your number one choice from the class top three list of the outplacement organizations for the Toronto hospital scenario and draft a report to your COO. Be sure to include your recommendation for the types of services you propose to purchase from the outplacement organization. Attempt to discover the cost of your recommendation for the hospital.

REFERENCE:

1. Dessler, G., Cole, N. and Sutherland, V. (1999). *Human Resources Management In Canada*. Canadian Seventh Edition, Scarborough, Ont: Prentice Hall Canada, p. 188.

23. IF I KNEW THEN WHAT I KNOW NOW: DISCRIMINATION IN THE EMPLOYMENT INTERVIEW

 LEARNING OBJECTIVES:

1.   To increase your knowledge of the "Prohibited Grounds of Discrimination in Canada".[1]

2.   To sensitize you to permissible and prohibited questions to ask candidates during the employment interview.

TYPE OF EXERCISE:

Individual Internet search, small group activities and class-wide discussion

RELATED CONCEPTS:

- Legal issues in HR
- Discrimination
- Canadian Human Rights Act
- Human Rights Codes for Canadian provinces
- Employment interview

 TIME: 45 minutes

Small groups will typically require 20 minutes in total to share their Internet search results and to complete the chart of questions. The class presentation and discussion of the questions will require 15 minutes. The debriefing will require another 10 minutes.

BACKGROUND:

The Canadian Human Rights Act entitles all individuals to equal employment opportunities without regard to: race or colour, national/ethnic origin, religion, age, family/marital status, sex (including pregnancy or childbirth), pardoned conviction, disability (either physical or mental or as the result of dependence on alcohol or drugs), or sexual orientation.

Section 8 of the Act reads:

It is a discriminatory practice,

(a)   to use or circulate any form of application for employment, or

(b)   in connection with employment or prospective employment, to publish any advertisement, or make any written or oral inquiry

that expresses or implies any limitation, specification or preference based on a prohibited ground of discrimination.

This Act covers employment in federal jurisdiction. Included are the various federal government departments and agencies, Crown corporations, airlines, banks, railways, interprovincial pipelines, radio, television and telephone companies that do business in more than one province.[2] The Canadian provinces have established their own Human Rights Codes under the umbrella of the Canadian Human Rights Commission.

This exercise will expand your knowledge of the prohibited grounds of discrimination in Canada in general and in your province in particular.

 **MATERIALS NEEDED:**

•   Two sheets of flip chart paper and one marker for each small group
•   One roll of masking tape

PREASSIGNMENT STUDENT PREPARATION:

Before the class in which you will be completing this exercise, search the following sites for information on human rights and the employment interview:

1.   The Canadian Human Rights Commission (http://www.chrc.ca/ http://www.chrc.ca/prohibit-motifs.asp?l=e and http://www.chrc.ca/screen-preselection.asp?l=e)

2.   The Human Rights Commission of <u>your own</u> province <u>and that of any one other province</u> from the following list:
•   Alberta: http://www.albertahumanrights.ab.ca/
•   British Columbia: http://www.bchrc.gav.bc.ca/
•   Manitoba: http://www.gov.mb.ca/hrc/
•   New Brunswick: http://www.gov.nb.ca/hrc-cdp/e/index.htm
•   Nova Scotia: http://www.gov.ns.ca/just/hr.htm

- Ontario: http://www.ohrc.on.ca and
  http://www.ohrc.on.ca/english/publications/emp_app_forms_eng.htm
- Prince Edward Island: http://www.gov.pe.ca/case/human/index.asp
- Quebec: http://www.cdpdj.qc.ca/
- Saskatchewan: http://www.gov.sk.ca/skrc/

3. The Ontario Human Right Commission (http://www.ohrc.on.ca/ and
http://www.ohrc.on.ca/index2.htm) Click on "Teaching HR in Ontario". (Many of the
other Canadian provinces have similar packages.) The package includes an HR quiz, Fact
Sheets, eight case studies and discussion questions. On the same page you will find a link
to the "Teachers Package". Click on this and you will learn the answers to the questions
posed in the "Teaching HR in Ontario" package.

Please make notes and bring them to class.

PROCESS/INSTRUCTIONS:

1. Please read the following scenario:

> *You are, Petra, a recent college graduate. Your area of concentration in college
> was computer science. You were delighted last year to have landed a job at a
> large Canadian radio station. Now, one year later, the owner/operator has asked
> you to assume some additional HR related duties because of your excellent
> "people skills". The station is desperate to fill the receptionist's position at the
> front desk. An ad for the position was placed in the newspaper three days ago and
> already you have a long list of candidates to interview. Since this is your first
> recruitment and selection assignment and you were not trained in HR in college,
> you are quite nervous about the upcoming employment interviews. To make
> matters worse, on the news today you heard about a complaint being lodged
> against the owner of another radio station in your province for violating the
> Human Rights Code during the employment process. You decide to call a friend
> from college who majored in HR to get some advice on what questions to ask and
> which to avoid during the interviews.*

2. Your instructor will divide the class into small groups. Share in general with your group
the information you found during your search of the Internet (see the PREASSIGNMENT
STUDENT PREPARATION section above) on the topic of Human Rights in Canada and
the provinces.

3. Everyone in your small group will take the role of Petra's HR friend. (The radio station is
located in your province.) You offer to sit and draft the questions with her. On a sheet of
flip paper (turned in the landscape mode-you will need at least two sheets), write the

following headings, one under the other, at the extreme left of the paper: age, religion, criminal record, disabilities, national/ethnic origin, height and weight, country of birth, religion/creed, family status and sexual orientation. To the right of this list, divide the rest of the paper into two equal columns. Label the first column "Prohibited Questions" and the other column "Permissible Questions". Please complete the chart by writing one permissible question (if there is one) for each of your headings on the left of the paper.

4.   Your instructor will ask each group to read its questions under certain headings. After each set of questions is read other groups are free to critique what they have heard.

DEBRIEFING:

1.   Have you or anyone you know ever felt discriminated against during the employment process? What did you do (or what did the other person do) about the discrimination?

2.   Is there much discrimination in Canada? What evidence can you cite for your answer?

3.   What are the best resources for someone like Petra to learn about human rights issues in Canada?

96

REFERENCES:

1.   Prohibited Grounds Of Discrimination In Canada; http://chrc.ca/prohibit-motifs.asp?l=e
        Reproduced with the permission of the Minister of Public Works and Government
        Services Canada.

2.   A Guide To Screening and Selection In Employment; http://www.chrc.ca/screen-
        preselection.asp?l=e

ESTABLISHING THE CONTINGENCY EMPLOYMENT CONTRACT

 LEARNING OBJECTIVES:

1. To understand the Canadian provincial and federal legal issues surrounding the employment contract.

2. To identify the critical elements of an employment contact.

3. To raise your awareness of the value of the employment contract.

TYPE OF EXERCISE:

Individual Internet research, small group activities and class-wide discussion

RELATED CONCEPTS:

*   Legal issues in HR
*   Federal and provincial employment law
*   Employment contract
*   Contingency workers

 TIME: 55 minutes

Small groups will typically require 5 minutes to brainstorm the benefits employers and employees reap from well-written employment contracts. The class presentation will take 10 minutes. The brainstorming of the elements of the employment contract is expected to take 5 minutes. Again, the class presentation will take 10 minutes. The sketching out of the contract for the consultant will require 15 minutes. The debriefing will take 10 minutes.

BACKGROUND:

The number of contract workers (also called: contingency workers, temporary workers, non-staff workers, and flexible staff) has grown exponentially in Canada in recent years as a direct result of corporate downsizing, restructuring and globalization. Many employers have learned the hard way about the value of having a carefully written employment contract with contingency workers. Michael Failes, Vice President of Governmental Affairs, HRPAO and a lawyer sends a wake-up call to employers about the necessity of having written employment contracts: "Every employee is employed under a contract even if it is only a verbal contract. Without a formal written contract, the job offer becomes the contract."[1]

Doug Burn, in an article entitled: "Courts Set The Terms If You Don't", draws a comparison between employment contracts and prenuptial agreements. He points out that both types of agreements specify a number of important conditions, duties and responsibilities for the duration of the relationship. Burn adds: "But even the most elementary employment contract or pre-nuptial includes terms and conditions for ending the relationship." For Burn, these termination terms and conditions are a key reason for drawing up an employment contract. He cautions employers that the terms and conditions stated in the employment contract must comply with both federal and provincial employment standards.[2]

This exercise will give you an opportunity to understand the critical elements that must be written into an effective employment contract and to understand the legal issues involved in such a contract.

 MATERIALS NEEDED:

- Two sheets of flip chart paper and one marker for each small group
- One roll of masking tape

PREASSIGNMENT STUDENT ASSIGNMENT:

Before the class in which you will completing this exercise, search the Internet for information on the following topics: employment contract (specifically, how to write an employment contract and elements of an employment contract) and federal and provincial labour standards (specifically, the Canada Labour Code, and employment standards for your province). You will find the following web sites to be very useful as a starting point for your search:

- http://labour-travail.hrdc-drhc.gc.ca/
- http://www.hroe.org
- http://www.minoritycareernet.com/newsltrs/96q4element.html
- http://smartbiz.com/sbs/arts/sbl2.htm

Be sure to bring the information you gather from this search to class.

PROCESS/INSTRUCTIONS:

1. Your instructor will divide the class into small groups. Within your group, share the results of your Internet search on "the employment contract". Brainstorm the reasons why a well-written employment contract would be of benefit to: 1. an employer and 2. a contract worker. Record your lists on a sheet of flip chart paper.

2. Your instructor will invite each group to present its lists. As each group presents, the remaining groups will stroke off any item that has been mentioned by other groups to avoid duplication.

3. Within your small group, brainstorm the elements that must be included in an employment contract.

4. Each group will be invited to present its list of elements. As in the step above, the remaining groups will stroke off any item that has been mentioned.

5. Within your small group, pretend that you are members of the HR department of your school. You have decided to hire an independent human resource consultant to conduct some training over the next six months with your administrative supervisors. Using the yield from your brainstorming sessions today and your Internet research, sketch out an employment contract (words and phrases only under headings) for your newly hired consultant. Be sure that your contract does not in any way contravene either federal or provincial employment standards. Your instructor will allow only 15 minutes maximum in class and then will ask you to complete the contract in full form before the next class.

DEBRIEFING:

1. Why should employers provide contract workers with a written contract? Why would contract workers want a written contract?

2. Why might an employer not want to have a written contract with a contract worker?

3. What are the key elements in a well-written employment contract?

4. What role do the federal and provincial employment standards play in employment contracts?

REFERENCES:

1. Burn, D. (1999, February/March). Courts set the Terms if you don't. *HR Professional*, p. 23.

2. Ibid., p. 25.

PART 3

HR SERVICES DELIVERY

JOB REQUIREMENTS

25. WALK IN MY SHOES, WHY DON'T YOU: EXPLORING QUALITATIVE JOB ANALYSIS TECHNIQUES

 LEARNING OBJECTIVES:

1. To understand the various components of a job analysis.

2. To highlight the different qualitative and quantitative methodologies for doing a job analysis.

3. To highlight the advantages and disadvantages of five qualitative job analysis techniques.

4. To practice planning a job analysis using a qualitative technique.

TYPE OF EXERCISE:

Small group activities and class-wide discussion

RELATED CONCEPTS:

- Job analysis
- Job description
- Job specification
- Recruitment and selection
- Human rights legislation
- Performance management

 TIME: 50 minutes

Small groups will typically require 15 minutes for discussion in class concerning their job analysis plans. The presentation of the job analysis strategy and implementation plans will take 25 minutes. The debriefing will require an additional 10 minutes.

BACKGROUND:

Job analysis ("the procedure for determining the tasks, duties, and responsibilities of each job, and the human attributes [knowledge, skills, and abilities] required to perform it") provides the data necessary for HR professionals to write the **job description** ("a written statement describing the duties, responsibilities, reporting relationships, and working conditions of a job") and the **job specification** ("a written summary of the requisite knowledge, skills, and abilities needed to perform the job"). Job analysis, "accurate information about jobs and their human requirements, which has been gathered in a gender-neutral, bias-free manner" has been termed the "cornerstone of HRM". Data gathered through the job analysis process provides invaluable information for decision making by HR professionals and others in the organization on key matters such as: recruitment and selection, compensation, performance management, HR development, human resource planning, labour relations, career development and job design.[1]

Job analysis is conducted by an in-house HR specialist or an external HR consultant in cooperation with the job incumbent and the job incumbent's supervisor. According to Dessler, Cole and Sutherland[2] the six steps in doing a job analysis are:

1. Identify the use to which the information about the job will be put, since this will determine the types of data that should be collected and the techniques used;
2. Review relevant background information such as organization charts, process charts, and job descriptions;
3. Select the representative positions and jobs to be analyzed. (It would be too time consuming to analyze every position among a cluster similar positions);
4. Analyze the jobs by collecting data on job activities, required employee behaviours, working conditions, and human traits and abilities needed to perform the job;
5. Review the information with job incumbents. This step provides verification and helps to win employee acceptance;
6. Develop a job description and job specification.

There are many job analysis techniques from which to choose namely quantitative techniques such as: observation of the incumbent at work, questionnaires completed by incumbents and supervisors, face-to-face individual and/or group interviews with the incumbents and supervisors, and diaries or logs completed by incumbents. Quantitative job analysis techniques include the following: the Position Analysis Questionnaire (PAQ) - a very structured job analysis questionnaire which is completed by a job analyst, and a functional job analysis - a job rating technique which classifies jobs based on types and responsibility for data, people and things and the extent to which instructions, reasoning, judgment and verbal facility are necessary for the various parts of the job. Performance standards and training requirements are also specified. In addition, there are many occupational classification systems in existence which can be of enormous assistance to the HR specialist in job analysis.[3] Canada's occupational data base which was compiled by the government of Canada "contains comprehensive, standardized descriptions of about 25 000 occupations and the requirements for each."[4]

This exercise will give you an opportunity to gain some first-hand experience with job analysis using qualitative techniques.

PREASSIGNMENT STUDENT PREPARATION:

1. Before the class in which you will be completing this exercise, your instructor will assign you to one of five job analysis methodology groups i.e., questionnaire, diary/log, individual interview, group interview or observation.

2. Within your group, research your job analysis technique by consulting a human resource text such as Dessler, Cole and Sutherland's *Human Resources Management In Canada*[5] to familiarize yourself with your assigned job analysis technique and to learn the advantages and disadvantages of your technique.

3. Meet with your group and plan your strategy for analyzing the job of a departmental secretary for your business school using your assigned qualitative job analysis technique. Design any instrument you would need to carry out the job analysis and write out any and all questions you would ask.

PROCESS/INSTRUCTIONS:

1. Within your group, review the advantages and disadvantages of your assigned technique. Discuss how you might minimize the disadvantages of your technique. Discuss which other techniques you would like to use in addition to your assigned technique in order to secure the best job analysis data. Prepare a 5 minutes report for the class on these deliberations.

2. Your instructor will ask each group in turn to report to the class.

DEBRIEFING:

1. What "how to" information did you learn during this exercise on completing a job analysis?

2. How would you combine job analysis techniques (qualitative and quantitative) to minimize the disadvantages of any one technique?

3. What is the best strategy for conducting a job analysis for the position of departmental secretary (administrative assistant) in a business school?

4. Does the position of job analyst appeal to you? Please explain your answer.

REFERENCES:

1. Dessler, G., Cole, N., and Sutherland, V. (1999). *Human Resource Management In Canada*. Seventh Edition. Scarborough, Ont.:Prentice Hall Canada, p. 127.

2. Ibid., pp 130-131.

3. Occupational Classifications Systems Review List; http://www.air-dc.org/ssa/air_ocs2.html

4. Dessler, G., Cole, N. and Sutherland, V., ibid., p. 140.

5. Ibid., pp. 136-137.

26. I GUESS THAT REALLY IS IN MY JOB DESCRIPTION: WRITING A JOB DESCRIPTION

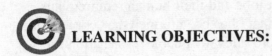

 LEARNING OBJECTIVES:

1. To understand the various components of a job description.

2. To understand what should and should not be part of a job description.

3. To practice writing a job description.

TYPE OF EXERCISE:

Individual Internet research, interview and brief written assignment - all completed outside of class

RELATED CONCEPTS:

*   Job description
*   Job analysis
*   Job specification
*   Recruitment and selection
*   Human rights legislation
*   Compensation
*   Performance management

TIME: 25 minutes

The instructor will require 10 minutes to make some observations in a class (after all job descriptions have been mailed back). The debriefing will take an additional 15 minutes.

BACKGROUND:

Job analysis ("the procedure for determining the tasks, duties, and responsibilities of each job, and the human attributes [knowledge, skills, and abilities] required to perform it") provides the data necessary for HR professionals to write the **job description** (a written statement describing the duties, responsibilities, reporting relationships, and working conditions of a job") and the **job specification** (a written summary of the requisite knowledge, skills, and abilities needed to perform the job). Job analysis, "accurate information about jobs and their human requirements, which has been gathered in a gender-neutral, bias-free manner" has been termed the "cornerstone of HRM". Data gathered through the job analysis process provides invaluable information for decision making by HR professionals and others in the organization on key matters such as: recruitment and selection, compensation, performance management, HR development, human resource planning, labour relations, career development and job design.[1]

Ernest Dale[2] the following guidelines for writing job descriptions: be clear, indicate scope of authority, be specific (descriptions of higher level positions tend to include broader responsibility statements than do the descriptions of lower-level positions), and be brief. Job descriptions must also be written in full accord with the human rights legislation in Canada.

This exercise will give you an opportunity to learn first-hand about writing a job description.

 MATERIALS NEEDED:

- A copy of the "Developing a Job Description Interview Form" (supplied by your instructor).

PROCESS/INSTRUCTIONS:

1. To gather more background information of job descriptions, investigate the following related topics:

    - What To Put In Job Descriptions
      (http://www.toolkit.cch.com/text/P05_0320.asp)

    - What Not To Put In Job Descriptions
      (http://www.toolkit.cch.com/text/P05_0360.asp)

    - Sample job descriptions (including job specification) for a Director of HR Systems with a global pharmaceutical corporation
      (http://ihrim.org/jobs/job_items/JW.html) and many other HR positions
      (http://www2.ihrim.org/jobs/JOBDE.html)

2. Each student must choose a relative or friend who is working full-time (preferably in an HR position, either in a managerial capacity or not) to interview. The purpose of the interview is to give you the experience of developing a job description for this individual's job. (Of course, you may not ask for a copy of this person's official job description!).

3. Schedule a telephone interview or a face-to-face interview as soon as mutually convenient. You should make every effort not to exceed 20 minutes in interview time. Complete the "Developing a Job Description Interview" form as you conduct the interview.

4. Using your interview data, write a job description for your interviewee's position. Deliver the description to your interviewee and ask this person to make a few written comments on the accuracy and quality of the job description. Give your interviewee a stamped envelope (which you have addressed to your instructor) and ask that he/she kindly mail the job description and comments to your instructor. Be sure to include your name on the job description for your instructor's information. Be sure to send a written "Thank You" note to your interviewee as soon as possible.

5. Your instructor will return the job description and comments to you in class and will make a few broad observations about all of the job descriptions completed for this exercise.

DEBRIEFING:

1. What "how to" information did you learn during this exercise on writing job descriptions?

2. Why might some organizations balk at writing job descriptions? Why should they write the job descriptions?

3. Why do some employees scoff at their job descriptions and say that the descriptions do not describe their jobs at all? What has gone wrong in a case like this in the writing of the job descriptions?

4. How do job descriptions for managerial positions differ from job descriptions for non-managerial positions?

5. Give some concrete examples of job description information that is in violation of the Canadian human rights legislation? How would you rewrite the job descriptions so that they do not violate the legislation.

REFERENCES:

1. Dessler, G., Cole, N., and Sutherland, V. (1999). *Human Resource Management In Canada*. Seventh Edition. Scarborough, Ont.:Prentice Hall Canada, p. 127.

2. Dale, E. (1967). *Organizations*. In Dessler, G., Cole, N., and Sutherland, V. (1999). *Human Resource Management In Canada*. Seventh Edition. Scarborough, Ont.:Prentice Hall Canada, pp. 146-147.

27. WHAT WE'RE REALLY LOOKING FOR IS...: WRITING A JOB SPECIFICATION

 LEARNING OBJECTIVES:

1. To understand the various components of a job specification.

2. To highlight what should and should not be part of a job specification.

3. To practice writing a job specification.

TYPE OF EXERCISE:

Small group activities and class-wide discussion

RELATED CONCEPTS:

*   Job specification
*   Job description
*   Job analysis
*   Recruitment and selection
*   Human rights legislation
*   Performance management

 TIME: 45 minutes

Small groups will typically require 15 minutes to read the Job Summary and write a partial job specification for the position. The presentation of the job specification will take 15 minutes. The comparison between the job specification designed in class and the actual job specification will require 5 minutes. The debriefing will require an additional 10 minutes.

BACKGROUND:

Job analysis ("the procedure for determining the tasks, duties, and responsibilities of each job, and the human attributes [knowledge, skills, and abilities] required to perform it") provides the data necessary for HR professionals to write the **job description** (a written statement describing the duties, responsibilities, reporting relationships, and working conditions of a job") and the **job specification** (a written summary of the requisite knowledge, skills, and abilities needed to perform the job). Job analysis, "accurate information about jobs and their human requirements, which has been gathered in a gender-neutral, bias-free manner" has been termed the "cornerstone of HRM". Data gathered through the job analysis process provides invaluable information for decision making by HR professionals and others in the organization on key matters such as: recruitment and selection, compensation, performance management, HR development, human resource planning, labour relations, career development and job design.[1]

The job specification spells out "personal qualities, traits, skills, and background required"[2] in order for a person to be able to fulfil the job duties and requirements. The job specification does not describe the job incumbent but rather objectively sets out the required specifications that the job holder would need to do the job effectively. Also included in the job specification are the following: effort factors i.e., physical demands and mental demands of the job and a description of the working conditions which are part and parcel of the job. The job specification must be written in full accord with the human rights legislation in Canada. The job specification most often found attached to the end of the job description although some organizations prefer to present it as a separate document.

This exercise will give you an opportunity to learn first-hand about writing a job specification.

 MATERIALS NEEDED:

- A copy of the job description(s) for each small group (supplied by your instructor)

PROCESS/INSTRUCTIONS:

1. Your instructor will divide the class into five small groups. Within your group, read the following "Job Summary" which is part of the job description for the position of Advisor, Human Resources (The Toronto General Hospital, dated May 31, 1996):[3]

   > *JOB SUMMARY: As an integral member of the Employee Relations team, the Human Resources Advisor is responsible for the provision of services and performance of responsibilities in support of the HR department and client groups to established levels of excellence, including:*
   >
   > *1.   providing guidance, advisory and consultative services to assigned client groups in support of the mandate of the HR department;*

112

2.   *ensuring the continuity of services to client groups;*

3.   *providing assistance to support the grievance resolution process;*

4.   *participating in and supporting HR projects and on-going activities;*

5.   *participating in the collective bargaining process, as requested;*

6.   *performing cross-functional duties;*

7.   *performing other duties as consistent with the job classification.*

2.   Your instructor will assign one of the first five job duties/responsibilities for the HR Advisor position to your group. Within your group, write a partial job specification for this position (considering your assigned duty/responsibility only for now) using the following headings: Education, Experience, Professional Affiliations/Memberships, Additional Skills/Abilities, Physical and Mental Demands, and Working Conditions.

3.   Your instructor will ask each group in turn to present its job specification <u>for the following headings only</u>: education, experience, professional affiliations/memberships and additional skills/abilities. The last group will be asked to include their job specification for the remaining headings i.e., physical and mental demands and working conditions.

4.   Your instructor will distribute a copy of the full job description (including the job specification for this position). Compare the job specification designed in this class with the actual job specification. (If there is time, your instructor may distribute copies of two other job descriptions for HR positions from The Toronto Hospital.)

DEBRIEFING:

1.   What "how to" information did you learn through the course of this exercise on a job specification?

2.   How would you assess each "additional skill/abilities" identified on the actual job description?

3.   Did anything on the actual job description for the position of HR advisor surprise you? Please explain your answer.

4.   Give some concrete examples of job specification information that might appear on some other job descriptions (obviously not the job description/specification you were given in class from The Toronto Hospital) that would be in violation of the Canadian human rights legislation? How would you rewrite the job specification so that it would not violate the legislation.

REFERENCES:

1.   Dessler, G., Cole, N., and Sutherland, V. (1999). *Human Resource Management In Canada*. Seventh Edition. Scarborough, Ont.:Prentice Hall Canada, p. 127.

2.   Ibid., p.127.

3.   The authors of this book wish to express their gratitude to Brian Flanagan, Director, Employee Development, Human Resources at The Toronto Hospital for granting us permission to reprint three job descriptions.

28. IF I DO MY JOB RIGHT... :
IDENTIFICATION OF JOB ACCOUNTABILITIES
AND KEY PERFORMANCE MEASURES

 LEARNING OBJECTIVES:

1.   To document job accountabilities in a position with which you are familiar.

2.   To identify key performance measures given the job accountabilities for that position.

3.   To focus on the "whats", " whens" and "hows" of performance criteria.

TYPE OF EXERCISE:

Small group activities and class-wide discussion

RELATED CONCEPTS:

- Recruitment and selection
- Performance management
- Job design

 TIME: 60 minutes

Small groups will typically require 5 minutes to brainstorm job accountabilities. The class
discussion of the accountabilities which will result in the narrowing of the accountabilities (for
purpose of further discussion) will require 15 minutes. The establishing of criteria for
performance measurement and the ensuing consensus discussion are each expected to take
10 minutes. Lastly, the small group discussions on measurement methodologies and training
requirements for supervisors on the topic of performance management will each require
10 minutes. The debriefing will require an additional 10 minutes.

BACKGROUND:

Several important factors that contribute to poor selection decisions are: the lack of proper identification of what is required in the role; the absence of clear and generally accepted critical performance measures; and the failure of supervisors to provide employees with feedback based on the application of the performance measures. All new hires need to know their employer's/supervisor's expectations and performance measurement details such as, who measures what, when and how. They also need to know that the measures used to evaluate their performance will be applied consistently, fairly and objectively. Well meaning and otherwise skilled people can fail in a job in the absence of an effective performance management system.

This exercise will help you become more familiar with two key areas of concern to HR professionals i.e., job accountabilities and effective performance management systems.

 MATERIALS NEEDED:

- One flip chart and marker for each group and an extra flip chart and marker for the instructor's use.
- One roll of masking tape

PROCESS / INSTRUCTIONS:

1. Your instructor will divide the class into small groups. With your group colleagues, brainstorm a list of what you consider to be the main accountabilities for the holder of the job to be named by your instructor. Elect a recorder for your group.

2. In round-robin fashion, your instructor will ask each group to read out and explain the job accountabilities listed in step 1. above. The class will then reach a consensus on three job accountabilities from all of those listed.

3. Given the three accountabilities agreed upon by the class in step 2. above, proceed to specify the criteria that should be measured to determine whether the performance of the holder of the job with respect to each accountability is effective. Be sure to give a complete rationale for each criterion described.

4. In a manner similar to step 2. above, the groups will share the results of their discussions on appropriate criteria for each of the three accountabilities and will then reach a class-wide consensus on which accountability (along with its criteria) will be further discussed with respect to measuring performance (see step 5. below).

5.   Identify the best method(s) for measuring each of the criterion you have described for the accountability agreed in step 4. above and discuss what type of training a supervisor would need to be able to use each of these methods effectively.

DEBRIEFING:

1.   Given the work you have just completed for this exercise, what would you, as a supervisor, tell your new-hire about performance expectations and management during your first meeting? Please explain your answer.

2.   What are the benefits for an organization in having a good performance management system?

3.   What are the costs to an organization of a poor performance management system?

4.   As an HR professional what training would you recommend first-line supervisors have in measuring the performance of their direct reports?

FOLLOW-UP ACTIVITIES:

1.   Do some research on the topic of "rater errors" in the literature on performance management systems.

2.   Outline the Table of Contents for a training workshop for first-line supervisors on the topic of performance management.

3.   Recall some of your own good and bad experiences with respect to the measurement of your own performance in organizations in which you have worked. Reexamine these experiences in the light of what you learned as a result of doing this exercise.

RECRUITMENT AND SELECTION

29. WHAT DO YOU THINK OF ME SO FAR?: REHEARSING THE JOB APPLICATION PROCESS

 LEARNING OBJECTIVES:

1.   To help you learn and rehearse elements in the job application process.

2.   To help you discover the opportunities and requirements of the contemporary Canadian HR job market.

TYPE OF EXERCISE:

Small group activity, Internet research and class-wide discussion

RELATED CONCEPTS:

•   Recruitment and selection

 TIME: 70 minutes

Small groups will typically require a maximum of 25 minutes to complete their search for the three HR ads and to choose one for the application process. The maximum time allowed for completing the job application process is 30 minutes. The feedback on applications will require another 15 minutes.

BACKGROUND:

The recruitment process is a complex dance involving mutual evaluation on the part of both the potential employer and the applicant. Both parties want to present themselves in the most positive light. The hiring process is crucial for any organization as a means of building and retaining a pool of talented human resources. Mastery of personal job search skills is crucial for every applicant.

This exercise offers you an opportunity to learn first hand about the application process and to discover more about the opportunities and requirements in the HR job market.

 ## MATERIALS NEEDED:

- Copies of the Classified Sections of two Canadian national newspapers.
- One computer (with Internet access) and printer per group.
- One blank disk for each group.

PREASSIGNMENT STUDENT PREPARATION:

Your instructor will ask you to bring to class a copy of the Classified Section of a national newspaper. Your instructor will also specify the publication date for you so that the class will have access to a wide variety of job advertisements from which to choose.

PROCESS / INSTRUCTIONS:

1.   Your instructor will divide the class into small groups. Each group will be assigned by lottery an HR specialty area (or generalist position) to research. Each group will search through the ads (in the newspapers brought in by students and in web sites as directed by your instructor) for three positions in the HR field related to your assigned specialty (or generalist) area. Make a copy of the three ads for each member of the group and one set for your instructor.

2.   For the three ads agreed upon by each group, discuss and compare the following information: duties, competencies required, educational accomplishments preferred, previous experience preferred, and size of the organization.

3.   Reach a consensus within your group about the one ad for which your group will apply. The group will apply as if it was one person who has completed her or his educational program in HR and ready to enter the job market. Draft a cover letter and design an imaginary résumé which emphasizes the requirements for the particular position.

4. Your instructor will ask each group to label a file folder with the name of the HR position for which the group has applied, and to place a copy of the ad and the completed application in this folder.

5. Your next task as a group is to assume the role of the person in the organization who will be reviewing the application (representing a different HR specialty) you are about to receive from another group in your class. Groups will pair up to give feedback to one another on applications as described in step 6. below.

6. Discuss the answers to the following questions: If your group was assigned the responsibility for hiring the person who will fill the job described in the ad, how would you rate the application in the folder? What aspects of the application appeal to you as a recruiter? What aspects of the application would discourage you from hiring this (imaginary) person? Offer suggestions to the "applicant" regarding ways in which the application could be improved.

DEBRIEFING:

1. Summarize the strengths and weaknesses that were common in many of the applications generated across the groups.

2. What competencies, experience and educational background requirements were common across most of the job ads you reviewed during this exercise?

3.	What were the most important aspects of the application process?

4.	How has your perception of the application process changed as a result of working through this exercise?

FOLLOW-UP ACTIVITIES:

1.	Based on the information in the job ad which most interested you during the exercise, speculate on questions you would expect to be asked in a job interview for that position.

2.	Invite an HR specialist and/or a Career Counsellor from your college's or university's student services department to meet with the class to critique the cover letters and résumés generated in this exercise. Ask this person to offer suggestions about key points to consider in the job interview process.

30. THAT WAS FAST AND YOU DON'T EVEN KNOW ME!: THE SELECTION INTERVIEW AND DECISION

 **LEARNING OBJECTIVES:**

1.   To give you the opportunity of making a selection decision.

2.   To stimulate your thinking about the important role played by interviewing skills in gathering rich information upon which to base a sound selection decision.

3.   To have you appreciate the folly of making important selection decisions based on scant information about the candidate.

TYPE OF EXERCISE:

Individual activities in "bear pit" fashion, class-wide participation and discussion

RELATED CONCEPTS:

*   Recruitment and selection
*   Selection decision
*   Interviewing skills

 TIME: 55 minutes

Choosing the interviewers, getting them established at the front of the room and having them brainstorm the required competencies for the position to be filled will typically require 15 minutes. Canvassing the rest of the class for additional competencies will require an additional 5 minutes. The distribution of the interview material and the first vote of the interviewers will require 10 minutes. The reading of the interview information to the class and the interviewers second vote is expected to take an additional 10 minutes. The class vote, the tally and recording of all three voting sessions and the receipt of further information by the instructor and the debriefing will take 15 minutes.

BACKGROUND:

Like all important, nonprogrammable decisions, the selection decision should be based on as much rich and relevant information as possible. While researchers have questioned the validity of the employment interview and 201 HR professionals, in a 1996 survey, gave the employment interview a slightly above average rating i.e., a rating of 3.49 and 3.42 for unstructured interviews and structured interviews respectively on a 5-point scale (with "5" reserved for an "extremely good" method for producing the best employees and a "1" for a method that was "not good"), one of the most popular selection methods continues to be the one-to-one employment interview.[1,2]

Employers believe that the interview in any of its various face-to-face forms e.g., nonstructured, structured, situational, behavioural description interview, or panel interview can be a potential source of rich information provided, among other factors of course, that the interviewer has the skills required. Poor interviewers, for example, waste too much of the interview time talking and not enough time in actively listening and truly getting to know the candidate. While the interviewer must spend some time giving an overview of the organization and explaining the requirements of the position, he or she must encourage the candidate to talk at length so that the interviewer can assess how that candidate might fit with the position and, further, how that candidate might add value to the organization and mesh with the corporate culture. If the interviewer lacks the requisite questioning techniques and/or active listening skills, the quality (and likely, also the quantity) of the information base for the final selection decision will be less than useful and will inevitably contribute to a poor selection decision.

This exercise will take the form of a mock interview in which the interviewer is forced to make a final selection decision based on less than rich information.

MATERIALS NEEDED:

- Five 4" by 6" white index cards, each with a different letter of the alphabet printed on it
- A roll of masking tape
- A small box or a hat filled with slips of white paper each containing a tidbit of information about the candidate (supposedly revealed by the candidate in a recent interview)
- 10 blank ballots (2 each for the five interviewers)
- Five pens
- A set of two 3" by 5" index cards (one green and one pink) for each student in the class who is not playing the role of an interviewer

PROCESS/INSTRUCTIONS:

1. Your instructor will ask for five volunteers from the class. The five volunteers will then be asked to sit in chairs at the front of the room. For the purposes of this exercise the five volunteers will play the role of independent interviewers i.e., each interviewer will complete the task without talking to any of the other interviewers. Each interviewer will be given a letter of the alphabet as an identifier. The task for the interviewers will be to weigh certain bits of information that supposedly were revealed to the interviewer in a recent face-to-face interview with the candidate. The position the interviewers are trying to fill is a senior leadership position in a large-sized manufacturing company which is in dire need of a turnaround.

2. Your instructor will ask the interviewers to brainstorm a list of the competencies that they would expect a candidate for such a position to have. A volunteer from the rest of the class will be asked to write the list on the chalkboard. Before declaring the list as final, your instructor will invite the rest of the class to add any other competencies they wish to the list.

3. Each of the five interviewers will be asked to choose three pieces of paper at random from the set prepared by the instructor. These pieces of paper each contain one "bit of information" which supposedly was obtained by the particular interviewer in a recent meeting with candidate. Each interviewer must not share these bits of information with anyone else in the room. The interviewer will then consider this information in the light of the nature of the position to be filled and of the competencies listed on the chalkboard. The interviewers will then be given a pen and a "ballot" by your instructor. Within the time limit set by your instructor, each interviewer will render a selection decision by writing the word "accept" or "reject" on the ballot, their interviewer identifier letter and the number "1". Your instructor will first collect these ballots and then ask each interviewer in turn to read out his or her three bits of information without revealing his or her selection decision. After each interviewer has read out his or her bits of information, the interviewers again will be asked to record a selection decision (this decision may or may not be the same as the first) in the same manner as before and to write a "2" on this ballot along with his or her identifier letter. Again, your instructor will collect these ballots.

4. Before announcing the decisions reached by the individual interviewers, your instructor will ask the rest of the class to render a selection decision which will be equivalent to the interviewers' second decision. This vote will taken by asking the rest of the class to hold up one of the two index cards they were given: a green index card means "accept" and a"pink" index card means "reject". Your instructor will record the results of this vote on the chalkboard..

5. Your instructor will now tally the interviewers' ballots and record the results by interviewer for each vote on the chalkboard. Your instructor will give you further information on the candidate.

DEBRIEFING:

1. Think back over your own employment interviews. Did you ever feel that an interviewer you encountered lacked the necessary interviewing skills? What did he or she do that convinced you of this lack?

2. Do you agree or disagree with the following statement: "Employment interviewers are in the first instance really searching for negative information rather than positive." Please explain your answer.

3. What is particularly realistic about this exercise? What makes this exercise seem somewhat unreal?

4. What are the potential costs of poor interviewing skills for an organization?

5. What are the advantages and disadvantages of the one-to-one employment interview as a selection method?

6. What are the advantages of using a computer interview as a complement to the face-to-face interview? In your opinion, will the computer interview ever replace the face-to-face interview. Please explain your answer.

FOLLOW-UP ACTIVITIES:

1. Do some research using the Internet and other electronic databases available by modem from your library on the topic of the employment interview, specifically:

   - What role is played in the interview by nonverbal communication?
   - How far into the interview does the interviewer get on average before he or she establishes a reject or accept bias?
   - How important is physical appearance in the employment interview in today's job market?

2. Compile two lists of references on the "how tos" of the employment interview i.e., one from the interviewer's perspective and the other from the candidate's point of view.

REFERENCES:

1.   Tepstra, D. (1996). *The Search For Effective Methods*. In Belcourt, M., Sherman, A., Bohlander, G. and Snell, S. (1999). *Managing Human Resources*, Second Canadian Edition, Toronto: ITP Nelson, p.173.

2.   Murray Axsmith and Associates. (1997). In Belcourt, M., Sherman, A., Bohlander, G. and Snell, S. (1999). *Managing Human Resources*. Second Canadian Edition, Toronto: ITP Nelson, p. 198.

ORIENTATION

31. OKAY, OKAY, BUT WHERE'S THE WASHROOM?: UNDERSTANDINGTHE BASICS OF NEW EMPLOYEE ORIENTATION

 LEARNING OBJECTIVES:

1.   To give you an opportunity to learn the "whos", "whats", and "whens" of formal, effective new employee orientation programs.

2.   To heighten your awareness of common errors made in ineffective orientation programs.

TYPE OF EXERCISE:

Small group activities and class-wide discussion

RELATED CONCEPTS:

- •   New employee orientation
- •   Recruitment and selection
- •   Management accountabilities
- •   Adult education

 TIME: 40 minutes

The small groups will typically require 15 minutes to complete their checklists. The presentations to the class will take 15 minutes. The debriefing will require an additional 10 minutes.

BACKGROUND:

Malcolm Knowles, a well-known expert on adult education, was the first to elaborate on the manager's role as an educator of adults. Knowles pointed out that adults have their own readiness to learn or "teachable moments". Some HR professionals and other managers have learned about these teachable moments the hard way.

Knowles gave an example of one manager who for years and years repeated the same orientation program "that had been worked out with beautiful logic to move from a history of the company through a review of the policies of the plant to a tour of the plant." The manager became increasingly perplexed when the new employees came back to him time and time again after being on the job for weeks to ask the same questions that the manager had answered in their orientation program. Finally, the manager decided to ask them what they wanted to know to get started on the job. He found to his surprise that questions about company history and policy came out only after weeks on the job. What the new employees wanted to know first were such things as: Where will I work? With whom will I work? What should I wear? etc.[1]

Many organizations have learned over time about the many cost-effective advantages of a well-thought out and executed orientation program for getting their new-hires "out of the gate" with a "fast start".[2] "Employee orientation provides new employees with basic background information about the employer, information they need to perform their jobs satisfactorily. ... Orientation programs range from brief, informal introductions to lengthy, formal programs."[3]

The following (and often much more) is covered with the new employee during an effective orientation process: information on the company such as key personnel, mission, vision, philosophy and values, personal information of interest to the new employee such as introduction to his/her supervisor and team members, benefits information, reporting procedures on a variety of topics e.g., time sheets, overtime, sick days, the rules of behaviour and conditions of employment e.g., hours of work and pay schedule, training overview and schedule and security and safety information e.g., keys and lockup procedures, safety procedures and rules.[4,5]"An orientation program [or the lack of one] can make an immediate and lasting impression on an employee that can mean the difference between the employee's success or failure."[6]

In most organizations, the HR function takes the lead in the orientation process. However, for a truly effective orientation program, a cooperative effort between line and staff is vital.[7] The benefits most often cited from an effective, formal orientation program are the following: lower turnover, increased productivity, improved employee morale, lower recruiting and training costs, facilitation of learning and reduction of the new employee's anxiety.[8]

This exercise will give you an opportunity to think through the entire orientation process from an adult education perspective with a view to avoiding the potential pitfalls. You will gain a better understanding of who should do what and when and why to orient new employees in the most effective manner.

 **MATERIALS NEEDED:**

- Two sheets of flip chart paper and one marker for each small group
- One roll of masking tape

PREASSIGNMENT STUDENT PREPARATION:

Before the class in which you will complete this exercise, search your school's web site (or the web site of another similar school) for any information posted on its orientation programs or a copy of its Employee Handbook. Make an appointment with the secretary/administrative assistant of your department or faculty (or any other department or faculty in your school) to ask questions about her/his job and about the orientation program she/he received at the start of the job.

Obtain a copy, read and make notes for class on the following articles (or parts thereof as specified):

1.   Birchard, B. (1997, September). Hire Great People Fast. *Fast Company*. pp. 132-143. Also available on *Fast Company*'s web site: http://www.fastcompany.com Search for "orientation". Read in particular pp. 142-143 re: "Get a Fast Start". The article outlines orientation ideas from Cisco's Fast Start program and MEMC Electronic Materials (orientation as a self-managed project) - both US companies.

2.   Mieszkowski, K. (1998, February: March). Get With The Program. *Fast Company*. pp. 28-30. Also available on *Fast Company*'s web site: http://www.fastcompany.com Search for "orientation". The article outlines orientation ideas from the electronic card company: Greet Street and from the well-known company Intel (two more American companies).

3.   Dessler, G., Cole, N, and Sutherland, V. (1999). *Human Resources Management In Canada*, Scarborough, Ont.: Prentice Hall Canada, pp. 301 and 302. On p. 301 students will find an orientation checklist from a retail chain and on p. 301, you will find a short feature on Toyota's orientation (and socialization) process at the Cambridge, Ontario plant.

4.   Belcourt, M., Sherman, A., Bohlander, G. and Snell, S. (1999). *Managing Human Resources*. Second Canadian Edition, Toronto: ITP Nelson, p. 214. Here you will find a supervisory orientation checklist.

PROCESS/INSTRUCTION:

1. Your instructor will divide your class into five small groups. Each group will be given a particular time frame within a new employee orientation program i.e., 1. Before the First Day, 2. First Day, 3. First Week, 4. First Month and 5. Before the end of the probationary period. Your new employee is a male and has just been hired as a departmental secretary/administrative assistant in the HR department of your school.

2. Within your small group, decide on what information your new employee will need at your assigned stage i.e., make a checklist, noting the following (be sure to mark the person's title on the checklist beside the appropriate duty/duties): who is the best person in the organization to provide the information, how should this information be communicated to the employee i.e., again, note the communication medium/media to be used on the checklist. How can you be sure that this information meets the needs of the employee? Record the checklist and other information on a sheet of flip chart paper.

3. Your instructor will ask each group in time sequence to present its checklist to the class. Each group which follows the first will need to present only unique points so as to avoid duplication of material.

DEBRIEFING:

1. What information does your employee need in each of the five time frames? Who is the best person to communicate this information? How should the information be communicated?

2. How would your new employee benefit from an effective orientation program? How would your school benefit?

3.	How did each of the small groups in your class show their awareness of Knowles' concept of "teachable moment"?

4.	What advice do you have for the HR department of your school about its orientation program or its web site (re: orientation in particular).

REFERENCES:

1.	Knowles, M. (1972, November). The Manager As An Educator. *Journal of Continuing Education and Training*, vol.2 (2), 97-105

2.	Birchard, B. (1997, September) Hire Great People Fast. *Fast Company, pp. 132-143.*

3.	Dessler, G., Cole, N, and Sutherland, V. (1999). *Human Resources Management In Canada.* (1999) Scarborough, Ont.: Prentice Hall Canada, p. 300.

4.	Ibid., pp. 300-301.

5.	Belcourt, M., Sherman, A., Bohlander, G. and Snell, S. (1999). *Managing Human Resources.* Second Canadian Edition, Toronto: ITP Nelson, p. 212.

6	Ibid., p. 213.

7.	Ibid., p. 213.

8.	Ibid., p. 212.

32. A PROFESSORIAL SCAVENGER HUNT: INVENTING NEW TOOLS AND TECHNIQUES FOR NEW EMPLOYEE ORIENTATION

 LEARNING OBJECTIVES:

1. To introduce you to a novel tool, the scavenger hunt, that can be used as a framework for an organization's new employee orientation program.

2. To inspire you to invent novel new employee orientation tools and techniques that can be useful and fun.

TYPE OF EXERCISE:

Small group activities and class-wide discussion

RELATED CONCEPTS:

• New employee orientation

 TIME: 50 minutes

Small groups will typically require 10 minutes to draw up its scavenger list. The class presentations on the scavenger list will take 10 minutes. The small group session on new inventions, the class presentations and the debriefing will each require 10 minutes.

BACKGROUND:

Organizations have learned over time about the many cost-effective advantages of a well-thought out and well-executed orientation program for getting their new-hires "out of the gate" with a "fast start".[1] "Employee orientation provides new employees with basic background information about the employer, information they need to perform their jobs satisfactorily. ... Orientation programs range from brief, informal introductions to lengthy, formal programs."[2]

The following (and often much more) is covered with the new employee during an effective orientation process: information on the company such as key personnel, mission, vision, philosophy and values, personal information of interest to the new employee such as introduction to his/her supervisor and team members, benefits information, reporting procedures on a variety of topics e.g., time sheets, overtime, sick days, the rules of behaviour and conditions of employment e.g., hours of work and pay schedule, training overview and schedule and security and safety information e.g., keys and lockup procedures, safety procedures and rules.[3,4] "An orientation program [or the lack of one] can make an immediate and lasting impression on an employee that can mean the difference between the employee's success or failure."[5]

In most organizations, the HR function takes the lead in the orientation process. However, for a truly effective orientation program, a cooperative effort between line and staff is vital.[6] The benefits most often cited from an effective, formal orientation program are the following: lower turnover, increased productivity, improved employee morale, lower recruiting and training costs, facilitation of learning and reduction of the new employee's anxiety.[7]

One interesting tool used at Canadian Tire Acceptance Limited in Welland, Ontario is the old-fashioned scavenger hunt. To complete the hunt, new employees are given a list of items to locate from all over the organization.

This exercise will give you an opportunity to design a scavenger hunt for a newly hired professor at your school. You will also have an opportunity to invent other new and fun orientation tools and techniques.

 MATERIALS NEEDED:

- Two sheets of flip chart paper and one marker for each small group
- One roll of masking tape

PROCESS/INSTRUCTION:

1. Your instructor will divide you into small groups. Your first task will be to design a scavenger hunt for a new professor who has just been hired in your business school. You want this professor to meet as many other professors, students and staff as she can across your campus, to learn as much as possible about your school and its students and programs, and to have fun - all in a time period of three hours. Draw up a list of items you want this professor to locate and where. Record your scavenger list on a piece of flip chart paper. Be sure to discuss and make notes on your rationale for each item (related to the criteria above for meeting professors/students/staff, learning about your school/students/programs and having fun).

2. Your instructor will ask each group in turn to share its list and to give its rationale for each item.

3. Your instructor will ask you to form new small groups i.e., no one in your new group will have worked with you to complete Step 1. and 2. above. Brainstorm a list of 12 well-known games. Discuss each game as a possible new tool or technique that could be adapted for use in a new employee orientation program. Choose your "most promising" game for further discussion. Develop a plan for using this game as an orientation tool. Record your plan on a sheet of flip chart paper.

4. Your professor will ask each group to present its plan to the class.

DEBRIEFING:

1. How can a scavenger hunt be used in a meaningful and fun way to orient new employees?

2. What cautions would you advise concerning the use of a scavenger hunt to orient new employees?

3. What were the top two orientation tools/techniques invented in class today? Please explain why you think these are the best.

FOLLOW-UP ACTIVITIES:

1. Write a memo to the head of the HR department in your school in which you tell this person about the exercise you completed in class today and in which you outline at least three of the new orientation tool/technique inventions from the class.

2. Invite the head of HR in your school to come to class to react to your memo and to tell you more about its current orientation for new employees.

REFERENCES:

1. Birchard, B. (1997, September). Hire Great People Fast. *Fast Company,* pp. 132-143.

2. Dessler, G., Cole, N, and Sutherland, V. (1999). *Human Resources Management In Canada.* Scarborough, Ont.: Prentice Hall Canada, p. 300.

3. Ibid., pp. 301-302.

4. Belcourt, M., Sherman, A., Bohlander, G. and Snell, S. (1999). *Managing Human Resources.* Second Canadian Edition, Toronto: ITP Nelson, p. 212.

5. Ibid., p. 213.

6. Ibid.

7. Ibid., p. 212.

PERFORMANCE MANAGEMENT

33. THE WHOLE TRUTH AND NOTHING BUT THE TRUTH: USING 360 - DEGREE FEEDBACK TO IMPROVE TEAM PERFORMANCE

 LEARNING OBJECTIVES:

1. To highlight the potential benefits and pitfalls of using 360-degree performance feedback systems.

2. To learn about the various applications of 360 systems.

3. To learn about design strategies for avoiding the potential pitfalls of 360 systems.

TYPE OF EXERCISE:

Individual Internet research, small group discussion and class-wide discussion

RELATED CONCEPTS:

*   Performance management
*   HR development
*   Team performance
*   Perception
*   Coaching
*   Leadership and supervision

 TIME: 55 minutes

Small groups will typically require 15 minutes to answer the questions on the 360 method of performance feedback. The crafting of the statements and the presentation to the class will take 10 minutes and 15 minutes respectively. The reaction to the instructor's announcement will require 5 minutes. The debriefing will require an additional 10 minutes.

BACKGROUND:

Along with, and perhaps in some ways because of, the dramatic increase in the use of teams in work organizations, there has been a "surge of interest" in a performance assessment tool known as 360-degree feedback or multi-source/multi-level feedback. For example, in 1997, one writer pegged the usage of 360 systems in U.S. organizations at 8 percent but added that 69 percent planned to introduce it in the next three years.[1] Another author more recently estimated that in the U.S. more than 90 percent of the major companies are using some form of multi-source assessment.[2]

The 360-degree performance feedback system is designed to provide feedback to an employee from various individuals who regularly interact with that individual in the course of his/her job such as team members, supervisor, customers, etc. Of all its various applications such as employee development, HR decision tool for promotion, termination or compensation, management and leadership development, perhaps the most effective is employee development. Provided of course that the system has been well planned, designed and implemented.[3]

This exercise will give you the opportunity to explore in depth the multi-source assessment system of performance management.

PREASSIGNMENT STUDENT PREPARATION:

Before the class in which you will be completing this exercise, research 360-degree feedback performance systems on the Internet. You should explore the following topics/materials (at minimum):

1. I. Debare's article on 360 reprinted from the *San Francisco Chronicle* at: http://www.sfgate.com/cgi-bin/article.cgi?file=/chronicle/archive/1997/05/05/BU65200.DTL

2. R. Nagel's article on 360 at: http://www.ipma-hr.org/global/360au.html

3. Con-way Transportation Services' first hand account of its own 360 system called "The Team Improvement Review" at: http://www.fastcompany.com/online/17/conway.html

4. Links to Performance Measurement-Related Topics at: http://www.zigonperf.com/Links.htm

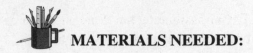 **MATERIALS NEEDED:**

- Two sheets of flip chart paper and one marker for each small group
- One roll of masking tape

PROCESS/INSTRUCTIONS:

1. Your instructor will divide the class into five small groups. Within your group, review the results of your Internet research by answering the following questions:

   - What does a "typical" 360-degree system look like i.e., Who provides the performance feedback?, How many people provide input?, Does the rated individual know who gave what feedback? What criteria are rated?, How are the results tabulated?, How is the supervisor involved in the performance system?

   - What are the potential benefits for work organizations and for individual employees of using 360-degree feedback?

   - What are the potential pitfalls of a 360 system?

   - Describe Con-Way's TIR system. How does it capitalize on the benefits of the 360 system and yet avoid the pitfalls?

   - What are the keys to a successful 360 system?

2. Your instructor will assign two of the following dimensions of team performance to each group:

   - commitment to excellence,
   - flexibility,
   - balance between task-orientation and relationship orientation,
   - trust,
   - participation and involvement,
   - support to team members,
   - quality of performance,
   - willingness to confront and resolve conflict,
   - candid and open discussion,
   - receptivity to members' ideas

3.   Within your group, craft three statements for each of your assigned team dimensions to be used as part of a 360 questionnaire/instrument. For example, if your dimension is "commitment to excellence," one statement could read: "This individual can be depended upon to deliver quality contributions." The following scale would then be used to evaluate a team member on this dimension:

Never   Rarely   Sometimes   Often   Always
  1 ---------- 2 ---------- 3 ---------- 4 ---------- 5

4.   Your instructor will ask each group in turn to present its statements. After each group presents, the class as a whole will be given a chance to suggest any improvements on each statement.

5.   Pretend that your small group is actually the group with whom you are working currently on group project for this course (or any other course you are taking). Your instructor will give you some additional information at this point. Discuss your reaction to his/her announcement. Translate the announcement into the language of a team in a work organization. What lesson can be learned from this about 360 systems and their applications?

DEBRIEFING:

1.   As an employee who works as part of a team, how would you welcome your company's decision to change from an annual one-on-one appraisal system with your supervisor to a 360-degree assessment? Please explain your answer.

2.   What are the best applications for the 360 system?

3.   What are the most controversial applications for the 360 system?

4.   If you were a supervisor responsible for overseeing the performance of a team, would you welcome your company's decision to change to a 360 system? Please explain your answer.

5.   Should your instructor adapt some of the methodologies of the 360 system into his/her evaluation of group projects? Please explain your answer.

6.   What are the keys to an effective 360 system?

REFERENCES:

1.   Debare, I. 360-Degrees of Evaluation: More Companies Turning To Full-Circle Job
        Reviews; http://www.sfgate.com/cgi-
        bin/article.cgi?file=/chronicle/archive/1997/05/05/BU65200.DTL

2.   Nagel, R. The 360-Degree Feedback Avalanche; http://www.ipma-
        hr.org/global/360au.html

3.   Ibid.

34. THERE'S SOMETHING WE SHOULD TALK ABOUT...: USING COACHING SKILLS TO IMPROVE PERFORMANCE

 LEARNING OBJECTIVES:

1.   To increase your awareness of the importance of coaching skills.

2.   To give your experience practicing coaching skills.

TYPE OF EXERCISE:

Individual Internet research, role play in pairs, discussion in pairs and class-wide discussion

RELATED CONCEPTS:

*   Leadership
*   Management
*   Influence
*   Communication
*   Employee relations
*   Stress

 TIME: 35 minutes.

The role play pairs will typically require 15 minutes for the role play and 10 minutes for the subsequent discussion. The debriefing will require an additional 10 minutes

BACKGROUND:

The effectiveness of an HR professional is measured by his/her ability to influence and support key employees. Often he/she is privy to personal information about colleagues. The ability to coach managers who are facing difficult circumstances can assist them to avoid potentially dramatic consequences.

Robert Hargrove has described a skillful coach as "someone who engages and enters into the learning system of a person, business, or social institution with the intent of improving it so as to impact people's ability to perform." He sees a coach as "a vision builder and value shaper, not just a technician who helps people reach their goals."[1] Coach Karen Whitworth describes the role of the coach as follows: "We point out the rock when they cross the river so they don't get their shoes wet... . We just ask questions so clients get their own answers; answers they are more inclined to take action on, instead of being told what to do."[2] Coaches help their clients to find fulfillment by regaining balance in the business and personal lives.[3,4] They do this by asking questions rather than by giving advice.[5] This exercise will give you an opportunity to experience coaching in a role play situation.

PREASSIGNMENT STUDENT PREPARATION:

To prepare for this exercise please visit the following web sites and read the articles mentioned:

- J. Kunkle, Changing For The Better (http://www.attractionselling.com/article_1.html),
- P. Luke, Coach's Lofty Mission (http://www.orca.bc.ca/pub/raf/Prov.htm),
- R. Hargrove, The Four Compass Points of Masterful Coaching: Mapping the Territory (http://www.smartbiz.com/sbs/arts/mfc1.htm) and
- C. Tristram, How to Find the Right Coach (http://www.fastcompany.com/online/05/coach4.html).

This material will give you different perspectives on the coaching process.

PROCESS/INSTRUCTIONS:

1. Your instructor will divide the class into pairs. Take a few minutes to read the following scenarios.

CLIENT SCENARIO:

You have just started a small web page development company and are working very hard to develop your market. You now have five staff working on consultation and web page development. Your clients are primarily small retail businesses in your local area. You are hoping to attract business on a provincial, regional and, eventually, on a national basis. You are married and have two small children. Your spouse is a partner in the business. Members of your extended family have been helping with child care but balancing your work and family life is a constant struggle. The business is running at a very fast pace and employees who usually get along well are becoming edgy with one another as they struggle to keep ahead of the demand. You have been taking orders from everyone who calls without narrowing your focus and staff are starting to express their frustration that they are trying to be all things to all people. While you are pleased that your business is growing, you are beginning to feel that you may explode if you do not find a way to reduce the stress soon. You decide to hire a coach to help you to think through the challenges that you are facing.

COACH SCENARIO:

You have been called in by the owner/manager of a small webpage development company who is feeling as if things are getting out of control both at home and at work. Your client is trying to build a business and cope with a young family and all the responsibilities that brings. Your client is concerned about the rapid growth of the company and the stress that this placing on the staff. The owner/manager is feeling at sea about life and work. Your job is to help this client to find a focus and build on past strengths.

2. You and your partner will each have twenty minutes to role play and conduct an initial coaching session. One of you will play the role of the client and the other the role of the coach.

As the client, you will tell the coach about your feelings of stress and confusion. You also will want to insure that the coach is well equipped to be of help to you so you. Be sure to ask how the coach plans to help you. Of course, you will want the coach's assurance that your conversations will be kept in the strictest confidence.

As the coach, your task is to ask questions such as the following that will encourage the client to develop a focus and to create a better life balance. Be sure to add questions of your own during the role play keeping in mind that the purpose of the questions is to help clients to develop their own intervention plans. The following are some "sample" questions for you to ask you client:

- Tell me what prompted you to start this business. What factors in your life contributed to the decision to start the business?
- Tell me about the times in the business that you have felt most happy and in control.
- Describe your vision of an ideal future for your company. What elements must be present for you to achieve this future? What strengths do you and your colleagues have now to meet these goals?
- Describe your ideal balance of home and work life. What resources will you need to achieve this balance?

3. After the 20 minute role play, discuss with your partner what other questions a coach may wish to ask a client in this situation. Discuss what additional questions you, as a client would want to ask a prospective coach to insure that the person is the right match for you. Discuss how, as the client, your perception of your life situation changed as you started to think about the questions the coach asked. How would this change in perception affect your business plan if you were the client?

4.   As a class, discuss the experience of acting as the client and as the coach in this exercise.

DEBRIEFING:

1.   For whom do you think coaching would be most helpful? Least helpful?

2..   Think of a time in your life when you felt stuck or overwhelmed. What questions could a coach have asked you that would have helped you to perceive the situation differently?

3.   Think of someone you know who in the past faced a challenging work problem. If you had been that person's coach, what questions would you have asked to help him/her to see the situation differently and from that change in perception, to have acted in a different way to solve the problem?

FOLLOW-UP ACTIVITIES:

1.   Interview an HR professional who works in a local business to ask about his/her experience with coaching. What are the similarities between the usual duties of an HR professional and the particular functions of a coach?

2.   Search the Internet for coaching sites that have been posted by professional coaches who are advertising their services. Compare and contrast the vision of coaching reflected in each of these sites. How does the image of coaching presented in these web sites differ from that of consulting?

REFERENCES:

1.   Hargrove, R., The Four Compass Points of Masterful Coaching: Mapping the Territory; http://www.smartbiz.com/sbs/arts/mfc1.htm

2.   Kunkle, J. (July 1998). Changing for the Better; http://www.attractionselling.com/article_1.html

3.   Ibid.

4.   Luke, P., Coach's Lofty Mission; http://www.orca.bc.ca/pub/raf/prov.htm

5.   Kunkle, J., ibid.

35. IT'S ALL IN THE MIX:
SETTING PERFORMANCE EXPECTATIONS

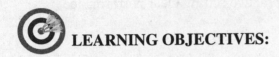 **LEARNING OBJECTIVES:**

1.   To learn the right mix of support and direction in setting performance expectations.

2.   To learn to take into account an individual's level of competence and confidence in setting performance expectations.

3.   To plan effectively for setting clear performance expectations.

4.   To practice communicating clear performance expectations.

TYPE OF EXERCISE:

Individual activities, two-person group activities and class-wide discussion

RELATED CONCEPTS:

*   Performance management
*   Delegation
*   Communication
*   Goal setting
*   Leadership
*   Supervision

 TIME: 45 minutes

Individuals typically require 10 minutes to plan for the delegation session. The delegation sessions will require a total of 15 minutes. The debriefing in pairs and the class-wide debriefing will each take 10 minutes.

BACKGROUND:

A critical component of effective performance management in organizations that is often not executed well is the setting of clear performance expectations. By not setting clear performance expectations, a supervisor runs the risk of wasted time, frustration and duplicated effort.

This exercise will give you the opportunity to plan and practice setting clear performance expectations.

PROCESS/INSTRUCTIONS:

1. Choose a partner with whom you will be completing this exercise. You will be delegating to your partner the task of note-taking for this class. Before you actually delegate to another person in the class, you will need to plan for the discussion and set out clear performance expectations. To assist you with your planning, please answer the following questions:

   - How competent at note-taking will my partner be? How can I find out?
   - How committed will my partner be to carrying out this task? How motivated will he/she be?
   - Given my answers to the above questions, how will I explain this task to him/her in terms of the performance outcomes I expect to see? How will I know when my partner does the task well? What will be my quality and quantity expectations for this task? How will I communicate these standards? How will I convince my partner of the importance of this task to me?
   - What specific resources (if any) do I think are important for my partner to use in fulfilling the task to my standards?

2. Sit opposite your partner and take turns delegating this task to each other (complete with performance expectations for the effective completion of this task).

3. Debrief with your partner after you have finished your delegation session by taking turns answering the following questions:

   - What were the strengths of the delegating sessions?
   - What were the weaknesses?
   - Did you feel your partner, as delegator, use the appropriate mix of support and direction with you?
   - Did you, as the note-taker designate, feel motivated to do a good job?
   - Were the performance expectations made clear in each delegating session?
   - How did you feel as delegator? How could you have improved the delegation session?

- How did you feel as the note-taker designate in the delegation session? Why? What assumptions did your partner, as delegator, seem to have made about your competence as a note-taker and your motivation to do the task? Was your partner accurate in making such assumptions?

DEBRIEFING:

1. What did you learn about setting performance expectations from this exercise?

2. What role does setting clear performance expectations play in effective performance management?

3. If you were a supervisor in a work organization, what would be the right mix of support and direction as you delegate to an experienced employee as opposed to delegating to a new employee? What leadership model might assist you in answering this question?

HR DEVELOPMENT

36. WOW! LOOK AT ME I'M A TRAINER: TEACHING CLASSMATES A SKILL

 LEARNING OBJECTIVES:

1. To provide an opportunity for students to test their own theories on how people learn.

2. To introduce HR students to steps in the On-the-Job-Training process.

TYPE OF EXERCISE:

Brief skill lessons taught by students randomly selected from the class and class wide discussion.

RELATED CONCEPTS:

- Operant conditioning
- Contingencies of reinforcement
- On-The-Job Training (OJT)

 TIME: 75 minutes

Your instructor will require 5 minutes to train the observers. Five students will be given 10 minutes each to conduct the skill lessons (minimum of five lessons = 50 minutes total). The reports from the observers will require a total of 10 minutes. The debriefing will take an additional 10 minutes.

BACKGROUND:

This exercise introduces you to the realities of the world of the trainer. This exercise will help you to grapple with the practical challenges faced by trainers and will give you an experiential context for the course material on learning/training in an organization.

 **MATERIALS NEEDED:**

- One 3" by 5" lined index card for each student
- Six "Observer Sheets" for the six individuals chosen, for this task (supplied by your instructor)
- One copy of "THE FOUR STEP METHOD OF ON-THE-JOB TRAINING: GUIDELINES" for each student

PREASSIGNMENT STUDENT PREPARATION:

Please come to class prepared to teach the class a brief skill lesson (i.e., how to tie a man's tie, how to do a certain dance, how to do a card trick, how to fold a paper airplane, etc. (Props are allowed.)

PROCESS/INSTRUCTIONS:

1. Your instructor will ask you to print (on an index card) your name and the name of the lesson you are prepared to teach the class. Your instructor will then collect the completed index cards and shuffle them in your presence.

2. Your instructor will then ask for six students to volunteer to be observers (i.e., these students will not be teaching a skill lesson but will, rather, observe each lesson and complete a structured observation sheet under the direction of your instructor.

3. Your instructor will ask for five volunteer "trainers". If five students don't volunteer, your instructor will then ask a student to choose at random the required number of index cards from the collected set.

4. Your instructor will give the class a 5 minute break while he/she trains the observers for their task.

5. The five trainers will each be given 10 minutes to conduct their training sessions. If a trainer has not finished his/her lesson in the 10 minute period, your instructor will interrupt and ask the trainer to outline what he/she had planned to do from that point on. The five training sessions will run back-to-back without comment from the instructor or the observers.

6. After the training sessions have been completed, trainers will be given a chance to "vent" their feelings. After this, the class members (other than the trainers and the observers) will be given a chance to express their opinions of the training sessions. Your instructor will then explain the task of the observers and will begin to reveal the true purpose of the

exercise. Next, the observers will give their reports one after the other. Your instructor will make some final observations on the training sessions and will hand to each student a copy of: "THE FOUR STEP METHOD of ON-THE-JOB TRAINING: GUIDELINES".

7.   Your instructor will pass around the complete set of index cards to abate curiosity on what the class missed by not hearing all the lessons.

DEBRIEFING:

1.   What were the prevailing assumptions by the trainers about how people learn?

2.   Reconcile these assumptions with learning theories and OJT methodology.

3.   Did the "learners" really learn? What evidence do you have to support your answer?

154

4. How would the class members (not the trainers and not the observers) improve on the training they received?

5. If you were a trainer during this exercise, how do you feel about your experience now that it is over? Do you think you would make a good trainer? Please explain your answer.

FOLLOW-UP ACTIVITIES:

Discuss the old adages:

1. "If the learner didn't learn, the teacher didn't teach."

2. "You can't teach an old dog new tricks."

37. PLEASE, NOT LIKE SCHOOL:
A MANAGEMENT DEVELOPMENT PROGRAM AS SEEN
THROUGH THE EYES OF AN UNWILLING PARTICIPANT

 LEARNING OBJECTIVES:

1.   To give you a glimpse into the uncomfortable world of the unwilling participant in a mandatory management development series.

2.   To give you experience in the application of the principles of adult learning in the design and delivery of a management development program.

TYPE OF EXERCISE:

Small group activities and class-wide discussion

RELATED CONCEPTS:

- HR development
- Principles of adult learning
- Program design
- Program delivery

 TIME: 60 minutes

Small groups will typically require 30 minutes to read the scenario, answer the two questions in Step 2. and share their answers with the rest of the class. A further 30 minutes will be required for distributing, reading, and applying the handout materials in Step 4. and to complete the debriefing.

BACKGROUND:

Not all adults have happy memories of their "dear old school days". For people who have learning disabilities that were not diagnosed (in the days before there was such wide spread awareness of learning disabilities), school may have been a source of frustration which prompted feelings of failure and rejection. Others may have had different negative experiences associated with school and school buildings. People who remember school fondly often forget that, even many years later, their former classmates may still be smarting from wounds inflicted by peers and others while they were growing up. These ghosts of rejections past can return to haunt managers and employees who are sent to mandatory training sessions.

Moreover, adults learn differently from children. According to Knowles[1], adult learners as compared with children are self-directing, have accumulated more experience, have a different readiness to learn and are problem-centred. Effective trainers and educators know the difference between pedagogy ("the art and science of teaching children") and andragogy ("the art and science of helping adults learn").[2]

This exercise will teach you the practical applications of andragogy in the context of management development program design and delivery.

PROCESS/INSTRUCTIONS:

1. Read the scenario below:

    Jack is a 47 year old supervisor in a large well-known, manufacturing plant. He quit school on the very day he reached the legal age. This was the birthday present he had dreamed about since he first began having trouble with his reading in grade two when he watched his classmates "getting gold stars" (as he called it) for their writing and oral reading assignments. By the time he quit, he was able to read only at about a grade four level, just enough to just get by. The humiliation of years of poor report cards had taken its toll. He promised himself from an early age that he would take charge of his own life as soon as he could. The day he quit school he wiped his feet on the school doormat as he was leaving, as if to wipe off the dust of hurt and shame of his unhappy school years.

    Despite his academic shortcomings, Jack had many other strengths which he put to good use from the time he was hired in the unionized manufacturing plant. His commitment to hard work and his ability to find innovative solutions to mechanical problems quickly got the attention of production management. First he was made lead hand and then later he was promoted to supervisor. He has been a supervisor for the last twenty years. His performance reviews have been outstanding over the years and his work group likes and respects him tremendously.

While Jack is very happy overall in his job, he does have some heavy personal concerns right now. His wife of 28 years, Donna, is recovering more slowly than expected from a stroke she suffered last year. To make matters worse, just last month, Jack lost a large amount of money in mutual funds and is having trouble meeting the mortgage payments on his aging house.

Today at the plant when he checked his e-mail he discovered that, in less than three weeks, he and 39 other supervisors at the plant must attend a management development program. The title of the training series is: Principles of Supervision in A Heavy Manufacturing Plant. The sessions are to be held in the conference room of the old hotel down the street from the plant. There will be five 3-hour sessions which will start immediately at the end of Jack's shift (4:00 pm for each of the five sessions). The announcement further indicated that all the supervisors are to complete "substantial" reading assignments before each session. Jack called up his long time buddy, Bill who is also a supervisor at the plant. If anyone knew more about this, it would be Bill.

According to Bill, the sessions would be taught by a professor who had never been a supervisor - much less seen the inside of a plant like theirs. Rumours were flying too that the production manager would be there for each session, that there would be a two-hour exam at the end of the sessions and that the supervisors who failed the test would lose their jobs! No one can figure out why on earth management would choose to start these sessions in just over two weeks when production in the plant is at an all time high.

2.   As soon as everyone has finished reading the scenario, your instructor will divide the class into small groups. Within your groups, please answer the following questions:

- What four things concern you the most about the upcoming management development sessions? Why?

- In what ways do you anticipate these sessions will be "like school" for you?

3.   In round-robin fashion, your instructor will ask various members of the different groups to offer their group's answers to each of the questions in turn asked in Step 2. above. Your instructor will ask student volunteers to capture the key points on the chalkboard.

4.   Your instructor will give you additional information to read at this point in the exercise. In light of the new material, your group will then discuss the following question:

- If the professor who will be teaching the management development series were to ask for your advice (you are still in the role of Jack) on the various aspects related to the design and delivery of this series, what recommendations would you make and why?

DEBRIEFING:

1. In what ways, could a trainer find out more about unwilling participants such as Jack before the training session starts?

2. What could happen if the trainer for this management development program were to face a whole room of "Jacks"(assuming the trainer has not done his/her "homework"before the program starts)?

3. How would you translate what you learned in this exercise about the principles of adult learning into a management development series that Jack would enjoy and would find useful in his daily work at the plant?

REFERENCES:

1. Knowles, M. (1972, November). The Manager As An Educator. *Journal of Continuing Education and Training*, Vol. 2 (2), 97-105.

2. Ibid.

 LEARNING OBJECTIVES:

1. To increase your awareness of the messages communicated to participants by the physical set-up of the learning space.

2. To give you the opportunity to apply the principles of adult learning in the design of a learning space for a management development program.

TYPE OF EXERCISE:

Individual activities, role play and small group activities

RELATED CONCEPTS:

- HR development
- Principles of adult learning
- Pedagogy and andragogy
- Design of physical space for adult learning

 TIME: 45 minutes

Individual activities will typically require 15 minutes. Small group activities will take
15 minutes. The instructor wrap-up and debriefing will require an additional 15 minutes.

BACKGROUND:

The physical design of a learning space sets the tone for any training session. For example, participants who enter a training room filled with chairs in straight rows immediately will get the message that they will be listening to the person at the front of the room and not interacting with and learning from their peers throughout the session. For some participants, such as the supervisor (Jack) whom you will get to know quite well during this exercise, this may trigger some bad memories from their long-past school days. A trainer who pays scant attention to the design of the learning space is missing out on a vital learning tool.

A key to understanding the important, if "silent", contribution made by the physical layout of the learning space to effective adult education can be found in the considerable works of Malcolm Knowles on "the art and science of helping adults learn" (andragogy).[1] Knowles was keenly aware that adults do learn differently from children. According to his writing, adult learners as compared with children tend to be self-directing, have accumulated more experience, have a different readiness to learn and are problem-centered.

This exercise will teach you how to apply the principles of andragogy (as opposed to pedagogy) to the physical design of a learning space for adult learners.

 MATERIALS:

- Three blank sheets of paper and one pencil with a large eraser for each small group (to be distributed by your instructor)
- One overhead transparency sheet and one marker per group.

PROCESS/INSTRUCTIONS:

1.   Please read the scenario below.

> *Jack is a 47 year old supervisor in a large well-known, manufacturing plant. He quit school on the very day he reached the legal age. This was the birthday present he had dreamed about since he first began having trouble with his reading in grade two when he watched his classmates "getting gold stars" (as he called it) for their writing and oral reading assignments. By the time he quit, he was able to read only at about a grade four level, just enough to just get by. The humiliation of years of poor report cards had taken its toll. He promised himself from an early age that he would take charge of his own life as soon as he could. The day he quit school he wiped his feet on the school doormat as he was leaving, as if to wipe off the dust of hurt and shame of his unhappy school years.*

> *Despite his academic shortcomings, Jack had many other strengths which he put to good use from the time he was hired in the unionized manufacturing plant. His commitment to hard work and his ability to find innovative solutions to mechanical problems quickly got the attention of production management. First he was made lead hand and then later he was promoted to supervisor. He has been a supervisor for the last twenty years. His performance reviews have been outstanding over the years and his work group likes and respects him tremendously.*

While Jack is very happy overall in his job, he does have some heavy personal concerns right now. His wife of 28 years, Donna, is recovering more slowly than expected from a stroke she suffered last year. To make matters worse, just last month, Jack lost a large amount of money in mutual funds and is having trouble meeting the mortgage payments on his aging house.

Today at the plant when he checked his e-mail he discovered that, in less than three weeks, he and 39 other supervisors at the plant must attend a management development program. The title of the training series is: Principles of Supervision in A Heavy Manufacturing Plant. The sessions are to be held in the conference room of the old hotel down the street from the plant. There will be five 3-hour sessions which will start immediately at the end of Jack's shift (4:00 pm for each of the five sessions). The announcement further indicated that all the supervisors are to complete "substantial" reading assignments before each session. Jack called up his long time buddy, Bill who is also a supervisor at the plant. If anyone knew more about this, it would be Bill.

According to Bill, the sessions would be taught by a professor who had never been a supervisor - much less seen the inside of a plant like theirs. Rumours were flying too that the production manager would be there for each session, that there would be a two-hour exam at the end of the sessions and that the supervisors who failed the test would lose their jobs! No one can figure out why on earth management would choose to start these sessions in just over two weeks when production in the plant is at an all time high.

2. Each and every student in the room will now "step into Jack's shoes". In a few minutes, your instructor will ask you to leave the room for five minutes. When you return you will be Jack who is just entering the hotel conference room on the first day of the Management Development series. Take a good look around, Jack, since no one else seems to be here yet.

3. Your instructor will ask you take out a couple of blank sheets of paper and a pencil. On these pieces of paper, you will jot down your answers to two questions which your instructor will pose in a few minutes. You may write your answers in point form. No one but the instructor will speak until both questions have been asked and answered (in writing). Your instructor will now ask the two questions.

4. Your instructor will choose two volunteers (one for each question) to go to the chalkboard and write while the rest of you share your answers to each question in turn in round-robin fashion.

5. Your instructor will divide the class into five-person groups. Your task will be to design a learning space which would be most appropriate for 20 supervisors (we'll assume for the sake of this exercise that the supervisors are very similar to Jack) and which would

work in a reasonably-sized hotel conference room. Your design will take the form of a labeled floor plan which shows the placement of tables, chairs, A/V equipment, etc. Be sure to appoint a recorder for your group. Ask the recorder to obtain three sheets of blank paper from your instructor (cut in the shape of the conference room), a pencil with an eraser, one blank transparency sheet and one transparency marker. Try out a few designs on the pieces of paper before you choose your final plan. Have your recorder draw this final plan on the transparency sheet.

6. Each recorder in turn will explain her or his group's plan and will show how the plan would answer Jack's concerns and would facilitate his learning.

DEBRIEFING:

1. How can the physical set-up of a learning space enhance the learning experience for adults? Please explain your answer.

2. How can the physical set-up of a learning space detract from the learning? Please explain your answer.

3. How can a trainer translate the principles of adult learning into an effective and pleasant learning space design?

FOLLOW-UP ACTIVITIES:

1. Invite to your class a professional trainer from an industrial setting similar to Jack's as soon as possible. Ask the trainer in what ways he/she feels that adult learners such as Jack are different from learners who are children. Ask the trainer to describe his/her preferred room set-up for the delivery of management development programs (similar to the one Jack is anticipating).

2. Visit one or more professional training facilities out in your community e.g., such as one operated by a bank or trust company. Note your feelings upon entering the room and the physical set-up including furnishings and placement of equipment. Ask about the various kinds of training activities are conducted in that room.

REFERENCE:

1. Knowles, M. (1972, November). The Manager As An Educator. *Journal of Continuing Education and Training*; Vol. 2 (2), 97-105.

39. LOOKING AT TRAINERS AND TRAINING THROUGH MY THIRD EYE:
AN EXTENSIVE INTERVIEW WITH A TRAINER

 LEARNING OBJECTIVES:

1.   To provide a vehicle for dialogue between students studying human resource management courses and trainers/educators in contemporary Canadian organizations.

2.   To present a comprehensive model of the Training and Development process and to provide an opportunity for students to test this model in contemporary organizations in Canada.

3.   To gain an appreciation for the eclectic backgrounds (educational and work experience) of today's organizational trainers and educators, and to examine the rewards, frustrations and concerns faced by professional trainers in all sectors of the economy.

4.   To give you practice in writing a reaction paper (subjective, opinion paper written in the first person using a conversational style "for the instructor's eyes only") in which you turn a "third eye" on your total interview experience with a trainer.

TYPE OF EXERCISE:

Individual interview (outside of class), individual oral class report, individual written report and reaction paper and class-wide discussion

RELATED CONCEPTS:

•   HR development
•   Three sequential phases of training and development i.e., needs analysis, design and implementation and evaluation and follow-up

 TIME: 15 minutes plus 5 minutes per student (distributed over two or three classes)

The individual class report will take 5 minutes for each student. The debriefing will require an additional 15 minutes.

BACKGROUND:

The training and development function, like its umbrella, human resource management, finds itself in dire need of reinvention as it prepares to enter the 21st century. Gone are the days of "training for training's sake", the rows and rows of thick, dust-covered training binders covering every imaginable topic, the fossilizing lesson plans and the piles and piles of completed "happy sheets" (short evaluation sheets which are filled out after each training event and then often not read).

Nowadays, trainers are caught-up in a whirlwind of personal goal-setting, self-development activities, discovering and furthering their core competencies, of seeking certification as training professionals, of linking in closer and closer to the vision and strategic direction of the organization, and of focussing on how training and development can add significant value and impact that is visible on the "bottom line". To do otherwise, trainers now know all too well, might mean that their function, like so many others in recent years, may well be outsourced.

This exercise invites you to visit a trainer and test out the well-established sequential and cyclical steps in the training and development process i.e., needs assessment, design and implementation of training, and evaluation and follow-up. You will get a rare, personal and meaningful glimpse into the world of the training and development professional. You will also gain an in depth understanding of the differences between teaching students in college and university and teaching adults on the job. You will see for yourselves how technological advances have changed the face of training and development (T&D) forever i.e., the advent of computer-based training, video conferencing, distance education, corporate universities and learning centres, etc.

PREASSIGNMENT STUDENT PREPARATION:

You will need to find a professional trainer to interview. You must obtain prior approval for your choice of trainer from your instructor before any official contact is made with the trainer. To obtain the approval of the trainer of your choice, you simply register the name of the trainer, the title of the trainer, the name of the trainer's organization, etc. on a sheet provided by your instructor. The purpose of this registration process is to avoid overloading any one trainer and to avoid duplication in the type of organization, e.g., the ideal mix of organizations would likely include a hospital, a large manufacturing company, a large management consulting firm, a bank, etc. You will be completing the following "Trainer Interview" form as part of this assignment/exercise:

TRAINER INTERVIEW FORM

INTERVIEWER:_____
                    Last Name   First

DATE OF INTERVIEW: _____

PLACE OF INTERVIEW: _____

_____

_____

DURATION OF INTERVIEW: _____

_____

_____

PART A - ABOUT THE ORGANIZATION

1.   Name of company or organization:_____

2.   Address of Organization:_____

   (please include postal code)   _____

_____

_____

3.   Type of organization:_____

4.   Size of organization: _____

5.   Head Office Location: _____

PART B - ABOUT THE TRAINER

1.   Name of Trainer: _____
                          Last Name   First Name

2.   Telephone Number: _____

3.   E-mail Address: _____

4.   Trainer's actual title: _____

5.   Job title of person to whom trainer reports: _____

167

6.   Brief job description for trainer:_____

_____._____

_____

7.   Brief description of trainer's career path to date:_____

_____

_____

8.   (a)   Length of tenure as a trainer: _____

        (b)   Length of tenure as trainer in this company/organization: _____

PART C - ABOUT THE TRAINING ENVIRONMENT/PHILOSOPHY

1.   Trainer's rating of top management support for training in this company:

2.   What evidence of support (or lack) of top management for training does the trainer cite?

3.   In the trainer's opinion, do students in school learn any differently from employees or managers in training programs in organizations? Please explain the implications for trainers in organizations.

PART D - ABOUT THE TRAINING PROGRAMS

1.   Describe any "canned" programs (i.e. purchased as a package) used in this organization. Indicate cost per trainee and evaluation methods used to determine the effectiveness of the program.

2.   Describe three of the trainer's current favourite training programs ("bought" or created by the trainer).

PART E - ABOUT TRAINING AS A CAREER

1.   What factors make the job of trainer complex and frustrating?

2.   What are the "rewards" of the job as trainer?

3.   What are the "key trends" in Training and Development today?

4.   If an additional $200 000 suddenly became available for training, how would the trainer choose to spend it?

PART F - STUDENT'S OWN QUESTIONS

Briefly outline your own questions asked during the interview. Please give a summary of the trainer's answers. Both your text(s) and class material should be useful for inspiration in this part of the interview. A minimum of six "discussion-type" questions are expected in this section. Feel free to add extra pages.

PLEASE NOTE: Student's questions must be separated from Parts A-E above and listed and answered in this section.

PART G - REACTION PAPER

In this section, students are asked to reflect on their interview, their answers to Parts A-E above, and all class material up to the class in which you share interview data and to write a four-page (maximum) reaction paper. This paper should be written in the first person singular and should take the form of a conversation between you and your instructor.

PROCESS/INSTRUCTIONS:

1.   Choose a trainer to interview from any sector (i.e., industry, business, non-profit, etc.)

2.   Ask for approval for the interview in class by registering with your instructor the name of your trainer, his/her organization's name, and other details as required on the sign up sheet. Your instructor will let you know if there is any problem with your choice. **For best results on the assignment choose a full-time trainer (if at all possible).**

3.   Thoroughly prepare for the interview by carefully reviewing the Trainer Interview Form before meeting with the trainer. You must also, thoroughly prepare your own additional questions beforehand. The trainer will no doubt want to have a copy of the Trainer Interview Form and additional questions before the interview. Perhaps he/she would be good enough to jot down a sketch of answers to these questions at his/her convenience before the interview. This would free you to explore your own questions in more depth during the interview. **Be very mindful of the trainer's limited time and other responsibilities!**

4.   After the interview, complete the Trainer Interview Form using a word processor. Your instructor will explain how you can get a copy of the form on disk.

5.   The final stage in the completion of this assignment is to write a short "reaction paper" (maximum of **four typed pages**) in which you explore the "fit" between the three sequential and cyclical steps of training and development and the training conducted in your interviewee's organization. **This paper should be written in the first person singular** and with a free flow of subjective ideas. You should write the reaction paper as if you were writing a personal letter to the professor.

You will be asked to share some of your interview data and thoughts about the interview in class. **CONFIDENTIALITY FOR BOTH INDIVIDUAL TRAINERS AND THEIR ORGANIZATIONS MUST BE MAINTAINED THROUGHOUT.** Your completed assignment must be submitted at the end of the class in which you report. The instructor will write a letter to thank participating trainers and will urge you to do the same as soon after the interview as possible.

DEBRIEFING:

1. What did you learn about the trainers themselves e.g., what is the "average" educational preparation of all trainers interviewed for this assignment? What are the most common frustrations among the trainers? How would the trainers spend a windfall of money if it came? What are the rewards for trainers?

2. In reality, do trainers cover the three sequential and cyclical steps of training and development. What are the constraints they face in doing so?

3. How different is the job of trainer in a large manufacturing organization from the job of an instructor in a high school?

4. Speculate about the future of training and development in corporations.

5. Would you want to pursue a career in training and development in Canada after graduation? Please explain your answer.

FOLLOW-UP ACTIVITIES:

1. Write a "thank you" note to the trainer thanking him/her for the time spent in the interview and asking permission to return after this exercise is finished to reflect on the experience.

2. Students who were fortunate to have chosen a particularly helpful and knowledgeable trainer to interview might want to ask the instructor to allow the trainer to come and address the class briefly as a member of a trainer panel. Such a panel held near the end of the course would serve as a final reality check on the usefulness of the course content.

40. WHY DID I EVER TAKE THIS JOB? : TAKING A SYSTEMIC APPROACH TO A TRAINING/CONSULTING ASSIGNMENT

 LEARNING OBJECTIVES:

1.   To give you a glimpse into the world of a novice trainer.

2.   To give you an understanding of the different phases of training and development in work organizations.

3.   To explore the systemic challenges faced by trainers in organizations.

TYPE OF EXERCISE:

Small group activities, role play and class-wide discussions

RELATED CONCEPTS:

*   HR development
*   Adult education

 TIME: 50 minutes

Small groups will typically require 20 minutes to read the original scenario and to answer the questions. The role play of the meeting and the debriefing are expected to take another 15 minutes each.

BACKGROUND:

It's not easy being a trainer/educator in an organization today. In some organizations where in-house training does still exist, misunderstandings about its purposes, processes and linkages with the bottom-line continue to muddy the organizational waters. The trainer of today is more than a training materials librarian, more than an author of countless numbers of thick training manuals, far more than an entertainer and more than a cure-all centre for all the organization's ills.

The trainer's world, like that of any business professional's, has been changed forever by the scores of new trends flooding through such as: the trainer as consultant, the learning organization, lifelong learning, total quality management, globalization, valuing diversity, cross-cultural training, emerging technology especially learning technologies, re-engineering and just-in-time training.[1]

Further, in-house training is seen by some managers as a panacea. Misguided managers such as these think that when they encounter problems, all they need to do is to call in the trainer and, magically, their problems will be solved. For managers who have this view of the training and development process, training content is prescriptive. For them training is like the old medicine, cod-liver oil i.e., a dose or two is good for a person despite the horrible taste on the way down! Trainers who are truly understand adult learning find this approach as difficult to digest as the cod-liver oil.

Malcom Knowles[2], a key figure in the development of a systematic approach to adult education, emphasized that adults need to be active participants in their own learning. Adults learners, unlike children in school, want training to be directly relevant to their day-to-day work. For this reason, adults are keen to learn material that relates to problems they are experiencing and tend to be intolerant of training sessions that force feed them irrelevant material. Instead, adults want to share their daily work experiences with other participants as they attempt to integrate the new learning into their existing mind set.

This exercise will give you the opportunity to step into the challenging, and often maddening, world of training and development and to see this world through the eyes of a self-taught trainer/consultant as she attempts to prove herself in a new position.

PROCESS/INSTRUCTIONS:

1.   Read the following scenario:

Janet is new to her position as trainer/consultant for a network of private medical care providers and, from the very start, is keen to show her flexibility and capabilities in meeting the considerable challenges that would inevitably confront her. Janet has no formal education in designing and delivering training programs per se but she does have many years of teaching experience at the high school level. She has a reputation as a gifted teacher. In the few years, after she left high school teaching, she has held several staff positions and latterly a supervisory position in a private medical care facility. Janet has an out-going and pleasing personality. She is seen as a natural for the new trainer/consultant position.

One of her first training requests came from a manager in one of the clinics. He had telephoned her to say that he wanted her to begin meeting with his staff every Friday afternoon from 4:00 p.m. to 5:00 p.m. for a period of six weeks in order to review the clinic's new approach to partnering with patients. Janet had met a few of his staff members previously on various occasions but does not know them very well. Janet feels very comfortable with the subject matter for this training series.

As soon as she arrives at the first training session, Janet knows she is in big trouble. The participants are polite but guarded. Their body language and whispered comments as they enter the training room clearly communicate their displeasure with this six-week "sentence". Even during the icebreaker activities there are irritated glances exchanged among the participants. As Janet makes her presentation, various staff members make muffled comments such as: "We've been dragged through training sessions like this every year," and "Having this on Friday afternoons is management's way of getting back at us."

Janet suddenly finds herself in a terrible quandary. As a new employee, still on probation, she realizes that she is being tested by management. As a professional trainer/consultant, she realizes she is working under less than optimal conditions.

2.   Join with any two other people in the class to form a small discussion group. Your group's task is to answer the following questions:

   - What's really going on here? (Hint: consider both the micro and macro perspectives of this situation)

   - What are Janet's choices at this early point in both her training series and her tenure in this position

   - Speculate on the underlying issues here for management? For staff?

3.   Your instructor will now hand two members of your group a different scenario/role on a random basis. Do not share this information with anyone else in your group. One member of your group will take the role of the manager (entitled: "Manager's Scenario"), a second group member will take the role of a training participant (entitled: "Staff Scenario") and the remaining member of your group will take the role of Janet. The latter will base his or her role as Janet on the information given in the original scenario in Step 1. above. Your instructor will also hand you some "how to" information on the training as a systemic and cyclic process and on the art and science of helping adults learn. Read this material and ask your instructor any questions you have about it. Next, the three of you are scheduled to meet in five minutes from now. The focus of your meeting is to address the concerns that you have identified in Step 2. above.

DEBRIEFING:

1.   In retrospect, what course of action should Janet have followed before the training sessions began? During the first training session? Please explain your rationale.

2.   What training techniques would be the most effective with these staff members over the course of the training series? Least effective techniques? Please explain your rationale.

3.   How should Janet evaluate the effectiveness of her training series (provided, of course, it actually gets off the ground!)?

REFERENCES:

1.   Belcourt, M., Sherman, A., Bohlander, G., and Snell, S. (1999). *Managing Human Resources*. Second Canadian Edition. Toronto: ITP Nelson, pp. 333-360.

2.   Knowles, M. (1972, November). The Managers as an Educator. *Journal of Continuing Education and Training*, Vol. 2 (2), 97-105.

41. IN LESS THAN THREE WEEKS, ARE YOU SERIOUS?: A TRAINER'S DILEMMA ABOUT WHETHER TO ACCEPT OR REJECT A TRAINING ASSIGNMENT

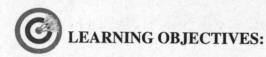

 LEARNING OBJECTIVES:

1.   To give you practice in decision-making in the role of a trainer.

2.   To give you experience in identifying potential pitfalls involved in designing and delivering effective training programs.

3.   To demonstrate the value of having an explicit or implicit comprehensive training model as a guide for designing and delivering effective training programs.

TYPE OF EXERCISE:

Individual activities, group activities and class-wide discussions

RELATED CONCEPTS

*   HR development
*   Designing, delivering and evaluating training programs

TIME: 60 minutes

Small groups will typically require 15 minutes to receive and process new information about designing and delivering training, to vote (individually - vote # 2), and to list the questions. The time required to share your group's information with the rest of the class and to vote (individually - vote # 3) is expected to take an additional 15 minutes. The final group activity and the debriefing will require 15 minutes each.

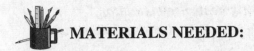 **MATERIALS NEEDED:**

- Four white, unlined and unpunched file cards for each student (supplied by the student)
- One class list with students' names in alphabetical order
- One flip chart pad and marker for each small group

PREASSIGNMENT STUDENT PREPARATION:

1. A day or two before you will be discussing this exercise in class, as directed by your instructor, read the following scenario:

    You are a senior professor in a large business school. In your ten years of teaching at this school, you have taught several different courses in the following disciplines: management, organizational behaviour and human resources management. Your teaching evaluations have generally tended to fall in the "Excellent" to "Very Good" range and are a great source of pride to you. You feel that your teacher training and the five years you spent as a teacher in a junior high school (ages 8 to 12) have been instrumental in your teaching success. For your first six years or so at this school, you felt you had your hands full with a very heavy teaching load and an advanced degree of your own to finish. In the last four years, however, you have heeded your Dean's advice to get more involved in your school's outreach programs, especially management development programs for local corporations and non-profit agencies.

    You have just received a call from your school's Director of Management Development Programs asking you to consider a request for training from a large well-known, heavy manufacturing company. She has some urgency in her voice and assures you that this would be a very lucrative contract for both you and your business school. Your "Dean" has suggested your name as the faculty member she should ask to consider this request. Apparently, the Production Manager called this morning with the hope of initiating a training session for at least 40 of the company's supervisors. The Production Manager provided the following list of specifications for the training program:

    - *The theme of the training is: Principles of Supervision In a Unionized Heavy Manufacturing Plant.*
    - *The sessions will be conducted in a hotel conference room.*
    - *The 40 managers will be trained in two groups of 20 each.*
    - *There will be a total of five 3-hour sessions for one group of 20 supervisors and then a repeat of these same sessions for the other 20 supervisors.*
    - *The first session is to begin 2 and one-half weeks from now.*
    - *The time frame for the weekly sessions is: 4:00 p.m. to 7:00 p.m.*

179

- *A text book and pre-class reading assignments are mandatory.*
- *Since production is at the "max" at the plant, no senior plant manager is free to come to any of the sessions.*

The Director has asked you to give her a definite answer (she says a "yes" would great!) by tomorrow noon. You find you have a lot of thinking to do by tomorrow. You recall that you have taught the principles of supervision to the large introductory management classes at your school for several years now. Further, after checking your schedule, you know you are available the dates and times proposed for all the sessions. And yet you still feel some uneasiness.

2.   Make a decision to "accept" or "reject" the training assignment and print your decision i.e., the word "accept" or "reject" on a white, unlined, and unpunched 3" by 5" file card and print your last name and first initial and the number "1" across the top of the file card.

3.   Hand the completed file card to your instructor at the beginning of the class in which you will be doing the rest of this exercise.

PROCESS/INSTRUCTIONS:

1.   Complete the PREASSIGNMENT STUDENT PREPARATION section above and hand the completed file card to your instructor at the beginning of class. Do not tell anyone what your decision was.

2.   Your instructor will give you additional information about designing and delivering training which is relevant to the scenario you read before class.
Within the time frame suggested by your instructor, you (as an individual) will be asked to again decide whether you would "accept" or "reject" the training assignment described in the scenario. Complete the file card as you did before but this time print the number "2" on the card. Be sure to remember to print your last name and first initial the card. Do not tell anyone what your decision was.

3.   Your instructor will divide the class into small groups. Elect a recorder for your group. List all the questions you would like to have answered before you would consider accepting the training assignment. Also indicate who you would like to answer each question, and the process you would use to get the answers to these questions.

4.   Your instructor will invite each group's recorder in turn to share the information from Step 3. above with the rest of the class. Without commenting on this information your instructor will ask you to again record your decision on whether to "accept" or "reject". Once again remember to print your last name and first initial and the number "3" across the top of this third file card. Hand your card to your instructor.

5.   Your instructor will assign each student to one of three groups, namely: A, B or C and
        will give each group further instructions and a time frame in which to work.

DEBRIEFING:

1.   As a general guideline, what information should a trainer have before accepting an
        external training contract?

2.   Identify the most important sources of information to which a trainer should have access
        in preparing a customized training program.

3.   What processes would you recommend for a trainer to obtain the needed information
        before designing a customized training program?

4.   Critically evaluate the additional information given to you in class by your instructor.

42. PLEASE LEAVE ME ALONE, I'M LEARNING: THE ART OF DEVELOPING AND USING LEARNING CONTRACTS IN ADULT EDUCATION

 LEARNING OBJECTIVES:

1.   To introduce you to concepts related to the field of adult education.

2.   To give you experience in designing a learning contract.

TYPE OF EXERCISE:

Two-person activity and class-wide discussion

RELATED CONCEPTS:

- Adult education
- Learning
- HR development
- Performance management

 TIME: 50 minutes

Each member of the pair will require approximately 20 minutes to interview the other. The debriefing session will take an additional 10 minutes.

BACKGROUND:

Malcom Knowles, a well-known educator, was a pioneer in the study of how adults learn. He differentiated between teacher-centred and learner-centred education. He described the latter as "andragogy", the art and science of helping adults learn and contrasted it with "pedagogy", the art and science of teaching children. The major differences between the two approaches are that: 1. adults can use their vast life experience in their learning experiences, 2. adults tend to focus their learning on meeting a particular informational need to solve a problem or complete a task and 3. adults are internally or intrinsically, not externally or extrinsically, motivated to learn.[1]

Learning contracts are one way these adult education principles can be put into action in organizations. These contracts consist of plans for participatory learning in which a self-sufficient learner develops a strategy to meet a set of learning goals. This approach has been used in colleges, universities, and in business. In a study with representatives of 27 Québec organizations, Roland Foucher, of the Université du Québec à Montréal, and Nicole Tremblay, of the Université de Montréal, found that self-directed learning, which includes the use of learning contracts along with other approaches, offers some useful options in the face of shrinking budgets and a rapidly increasing need for training and development in work organizations.[2]

This exercise will introduce you to the process of developing a learning contract.

PREASSIGNMENT STUDENT PREPARATION:

Before the class in which you will be completing this exercise, identify one skill you want to learn that is related to your academic program or , if you are employed, to your work.

PROCESS/INSTRUCTIONS:

1. Choose a partner in your class with whom you would like to work on this exercise.

2. Share with your partner the skill you identified (in the PREASSIGNMENT STUDENT PREPARATION section) that you would like to learn that is related to your academic program or, if you are employed, to your work.

3. Using the learning contract form that is provided for you, interview your partner concerning the skill he/she wishes to develop. The job of the interviewer is to prompt the interviewee to think carefully about each aspect of the learning contract to insure that it is complete, that all aspects of the contract relate to the learning objectives and that the contract is "doable"/practical. Be sure to complete all aspects of the form in sufficient detail so your partner has a complete learning contract at the end of the interview.

LEARNING CONTRACT FORM

(Based on Developing Your Learning Contract, University College of the Fraser Valley,
http://www.uctv.bc.ca/adedGISInst.htm)

1.   NAME:

2.   DESCRIPTION OF SKILL TO BE LEARNED (e.g., I intend to learn how to develop,
      execute and evaluate a training program in a human services organization.):

3.   IDENTIFY HOW THIS SKILL RELATES TO YOUR ACADEMIC WORK OR TO
      YOUR EMPLOYMENT (e.g. I work as an HR professional in a hospital and want to
      improve my training skills.):

4.   LIST LEARNING OBJECTIVES (e.g. To develop a comprehensive training plan for a
      human services organization):

5. LIST AND DESCRIBE THE LEARNING ACTIVITIES YOU WILL USE TO ACHIEVE THESE OBJECTIVES (e.g.: I will interview an HR practitioner about the methods they use to identify employees' skill levels):

6. LIST THE METHODS/PRODUCTS YOU WILL USE TO DEMONSTRATE YOUR LEARNING (e.g.: I will develop a sample training needs assessment inventory to be used in a human services organization):

7. SPECIFY THE TIME YOU WILL NEED TO COMPLETE THE ITEMS THAT WILL DEMONSTRATE YOUR LEARNING:

8. IDENTIFY THE PERSON WHO WILL REVIEW YOUR LEARNING PRODUCTS:

4.   When you have completed your interview and contract development process with your
        partner, he/she will interview you about the skill you want to master. Be sure to
        complete each aspect of the contract as you did with your partner in Step 3. above.

DEBRIEFING:

1.   Why would a learning contract not be appropriate for children?

2.   Why is a learning contract a valuable tool for adult education?

3.   In what specific situations in the work organization could a learning contract be used
        effectively?

4.   What were the most challenging aspects of designing the learning contract? What
        impressions will you take away from this exercise?

5.   What would you consider to be the strengths and weaknesses of the self-directed learning contract in comparison with more traditional learning formats such as college or university classes? Where in your school could learning contracts be used effectively?

FOLLOW-UP ACTIVITIES:

1.   Follow the plan you developed in the learning contract and report back to your interview partner and/or your instructor on your progress throughout the semester.

2.   Interview a professional trainer who helps his/her clients to develop learning contracts.

REFERENCES:

1.   Imel, S. Guidelines for Working with Adult Learners. ERIC Digest No. 154; http://www.ed.gov/databases/ERIC_Digests/ed377313.html

2.   Foucher, R. and Tremblay, N. (1992). Self-Directed Learning in the Workplace: A Framework for Analysis; http://artsci-ccwin.concordia.ca/education/girat/fouchertra.html

CAREER DEVELOPMENT

43. IT'S CRUNCH TIME FOR MY CAREER PLAN: DEVELOPING A PERSONAL CAREER PLAN [1]

 LEARNING OBJECTIVES:

1.   To assist you as you begin a personal career plan.

2.   To provide you with the knowledge to coach others in career planning.

3.   To make you aware of the benefits of having a personal career plan.

TYPE OF EXERCISE:

Individual activities and class-wide discussion

RELATED CONCEPTS:

- Career planning
- Goal setting
- Recruitment and selection

 TIME: 15 minutes

The class-wide discussion including the debriefing will typically require 15 minutes.

PREASSIGNMENT STUDENT PREPARATION:

Before the class in which you will be completing this exercise, please answer the following three sets of questions:

- Set One: Personal Assessment:

    - What special skills do you have now that you could bring to a job?

    - In what ways do you believe you could add value to an organization which would want to hire you?
    - Based on your work-related or school-related experience and feedback, what are your most serious weaknesses or limitations?

    - Think back to all your previous work experiences. What type of work/job did you most enjoy doing? What elements of the all the jobs you have had did you enjoy the most? (If you have not had work experience yet, what type of work do you think you would enjoy most? Why?)

    - What types of jobs do you think you would like to do that would incorporate some of the elements from the previous question?

    - To what extent do the jobs you've listed above require the skills you identified in the first question above? To what extent do the jobs you've listed above require some of the skills/characteristics which you identified as a weakness or limitation for you in the second question (in this set of questions)?

- Set Two: Opportunities Analysis:

    - Are there lots of opportunities for the jobs you've identified as being of special interest to you?

    - Are these job opportunities available within the geographical locations in which you are interested?

    - What will the requirements for these jobs in 2 years? In 5 years?

    - If you didn't know the answers to any of the questions in this set, where could you go to find out more information of this type?

189

- Set Three: Career Objectives:

    - What are your career goals for the short term i.e., up to one year from now?

    - What are your longer term goals i.e., three to five years from now?

PROCESS/INSTRUCTIONS:

Your instructor will facilitate a general discussion on the topic of career planning.

DEBRIEFING:

1. Why should you begin now to write a personal career plan?

2. How difficult was it for you to answer the questions posed in Set One (Personal Assessment)? Please explain your answer.

3. Did you have any difficulty answering the questions posed in Set Two (Opportunities Analysis)? Please explain your answer.

4.   What resources can you identify that would give you more information to assist you with the Opportunities Analysis (Set Two)?

5.   How difficult was it for you to identify your longer term career goals in Set Three? Please explain your answer.

REFERENCE:

1.   This exercise has been adapted from Greenberg, J., Baron, R.A., Sales, C.A. and Owen, F.A. (1996). *Behaviour in Organizations*. Canadian Edition. Scarborough, Ontario: Prentice Hall Canada, pp. 223-224.

44. "BRAND YOU"[1]:
CAREER DEVELOPMENT MEETS THE 21st CENTURY

 LEARNING OBJECTIVES:

1.   To sensitize students to the impact of the "new" workforce on the career objectives and career path of new graduates.

2.   To explore the "brand" concept as it relates to you as a future employee i.e., "Brand You".

3.   To explore the potential impact of the "Brand You" concept on organizations.

TYPE OF EXERCISE:

Individual activities, small group activities and class-wide discussion

RELATED CONCEPTS:

- Career development
- HR and organizational trends analysis
- HR strategy development
- Reward and recognition

 TIME: 50 minutes

Small groups will typically require 20 minutes to critique the Peters' article and share Brand Equity Evaluation results. The drawing up of the positive and negative impacts lists and merging the results into master lists will require another 15 minutes. The debriefing session will require a minimum of 15 minutes.

BACKGROUND:

In an article in *Fast Company* magazine (see web site: www.brandyou.com), Tom Peters makes the case for developing your image as a brand, "Brand You". Peters challenges employees to ask themselves a critical question, "What is it that my product or service does that makes it different?"[2] He recognizes that this question is a very tough one and that it requires demands a big adjustment in thinking. It requires that employees stop thinking of themselves as employees and start thinking of themselves as a brand. Peters advises them in his article: "You're not defined by your job title and you're not confined by your job description." He argues that they should set aside their job title as a description of what they do and, instead, implores them: "Ask yourself: What do I do that adds remarkable, measurable, distinguished and distinctive value?"[3]

From the perspective of HR professionals, the implications of Peters' thesis are considerable. The old days of a person's being hired by a company right out of college or university and then staying with that company for the rest of his or her working life are long gone. Instead, people entering the workforce in the 21st century can expect to have multiple careers and multiple organizational affiliations. To thrive in this competitive and fast-changing environment, each individual must be committed to continuous learning and self-promotion. Organizations that provide opportunities for multiple skill development tend to be more attractive than organizations that offer employees a traditional "job box" with limited access to new challenges.

 MATERIALS NEEDED:

- One copy of the article entitled: "The Brand Called You" by Tom Peters (August-September 1997). *Fast Company.* pp. 83-94 per student.

PREASSIGNMENT STUDENT PREPARATION:

Locate and read the article: "The Brand Called You" by Tom Peters (as referenced above). Apply Peters' message to yourself by reflecting on the nature of our personal "brand" of knowledge, competencies, and personal qualities that could add value to a particular project or company. Complete Peters' Brand Equity Evaluation questionnaire which is printed as part of the article. Be sure to bring your copy of the article and your Brand Equity Evaluation results to class.

PROCESS/INSTRUCTIONS:

1. Divide into small groups and ask each member to give his or her critique of the Peters' Brand You article and to share, on a voluntary basis, his or her results from the Brand Equity Evaluation. Determine if there is a general "buy-in" to the Brand You concept in your group. Your instructor will sit in with each group for a few minutes in order to learn the tenor of each group's discussion (and eventually the whole class).

2.   Your next task will be to discuss either the potential positive impacts OR the potential negative impacts on organizations if and when the majority of employees shift from loyalty to their company to loyalty to their own "brand". Your instructor will assign your group to the positive impacts side or the negative impacts side. Within the given time limit, brainstorm as many impacts as you can.

3.   All of the "positive" groups will join together to integrate and rationalize their lists into one master list. The "negative" groups will do the same. These master lists will then be photocopied for each member of the class. A short time (as specified by your instructor) will be set aside to ask for clarification or to challenge the information on the master lists.

DEBRIEFING:

1.   In your opinion, will the "Brand You" concept really catch on in the work organizations of the 21st century or is it here now?

2.   Is it possible to have a strong sense of loyalty both to your organization and to yourself as an individual "brand"?

3.   Discuss the implications of an inter-generational conflict between baby boom managers and the so-called Generation X and Generation Y workers who are developing their own "brand" identity.

FOLLOW-UP ACTIVITIES:

1. Search out Statistics Canada figures on the number of jobs the average Canadian can expect to have in an average 21st century career.

2. Invite a career counselling professional to come to class to give his/her perspective on the Brand You concept and its likely impact of organizations in the 21st century and/or to make a presentation to the class on the basic skills needed for the job search process.

REFERENCES:

1. Peters, T. (1997, August - September). The Brand Called You. *Fast Company*. pp. 83-94., quote p. 86.

2. Ibid., p.86.

3. Ibid.

45. THE "ELEGANT CURRENCY" OF MENTORING: LOOKING AT MENTORING FROM ALL SIDES

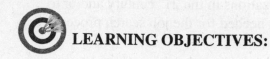 **LEARNING OBJECTIVES:**

1. To facilitate your investigation into the topic of mentoring as a career development tool.

2. To learn the advantages of mentoring for both mentors and protégés.

3. To learn the potential pitfalls in mentoring programs.

4. To discover the "tricks of the trade" of mentoring by amassing your own virtual library.

TYPE OF EXERCISE:

Individual Internet research, small group activities, and class-wide discussion

RELATED CONCEPTS:

- Mentoring
- HR development
- Career development
- Learning
- Person-job fit
- Adult education

 TIME: 40 minutes

Small groups will typically require 15 minutes to consolidate their answers to assigned questions. The class-wide reporting of the answers will take 15 minutes. The debriefing will require an additional 10 minutes.

BACKGROUND:

California-based organization consultant, Dr. Beverly Kaye, says today's mentoring is all about "learning to reciprocate" - as she calls it - "elegant currency". To demonstrate what she means, Dr. Kaye relates an example of the time a graduate student telephoned her asking if she would grant the student a 30-minute interview. In exchange for her time, the student offered her two hours of Internet research. The chance to fulfil each other's needs immediately got Dr. Kaye's attention.[1]

To Dr. Kaye, mentoring is a golden opportunity to learn from everyone in the company, not just those above in the hierarchy. "Mentoring is no longer just the grizzled old warrior having lunch a few times a year with the upcoming star. ... But in today's fast-paced and flatter companies, mentoring serves a host of other purposes, from retaining good staff to communicating across business lines."[2]

This exercise will give you the opportunity to explore the advantages and potential pitfalls of mentoring from the perspective of the organization, the mentor and the protégé.

 MATERIALS NEEDED:

- Three sheets of flip chart paper and one marker for each small group
- One roll of masking tape

PREASSIGNMENT STUDENT PREPARATION:

Before the class in which you will be completing this exercise, your instructor will divide the class into small groups and will assign certain questions from the list below to each group. Each group member is expected to research the answers to her/his assigned questions on the Internet. Your instructor will give you a list of useful web sites to get you started. Please feel free to search for material beyond that found on the sites supplied by your instructor. The complete set of questions is as follows:

1. What is mentoring?
2. What are the purposes for which mentoring programs are established in organizations beyond career development?
3. What are the old myths and new realities of mentoring?
4. What is in it for mentors?
5. What is in it for protégés?
6. What roles do good mentors play?
7. What are the pitfalls that can sabotage mentorship programs in organizations?
8. Do men and women mentor differently?
9. Is "group mentoring" a viable option for contemporary organizations?

10. What are the keys to building a successful mentorship program in an organization?
11. Which companies have successful mentorship programs?
12. What web sites (excluding those given to you by your instructor) did you find were most informative on the topic of mentoring?

PROCESS/INSTRUCTIONS:

1. In your pre-assigned small group, pool your answers to your assigned questions. Record a complete answer to each question on flip chart paper.

2. Your instructor will ask each group to present its answers in turn. As each group presents, its flip chart record will be posted on the chalkboard.

DEBRIEFING:

1. What are the benefits to the organization, the mentor and the protégé of an effective mentoring program?

2. Why do some mentoring programs fail?

3. What are the key elements of an effective mentoring program?

198

4.   How have mentoring programs changed over the years? Why have they changed?

5.   How does effective group mentoring work?

FOLLOW-UP ACTIVITIES:

1.   Find four other class colleagues who would like to experience mentoring first-hand. Meet together with your instructor and discuss the following:

- Who (a member of the HR profession) could you (the group) get to be your mentor? How will you establish the first contact? What can you offer the mentor as your part of the "elegant currency"?

- What do you want to learn specifically from the mentor e.g., what the HR professional's job entails, how you might fit into the HR professional's world, how to work with other HR professionals in the HR department, etc.

- What structural guidelines do you suggest for the relationship e.g., how often you should meet together, how long the relationship should last, what expectations each has for the other in the relationship, etc.

Your instructor will ask the group to make a report to the rest of the class on your group mentoring experience.

2.   Invite representatives from a few companies/organizations which are operating successful mentoring programs at the present time.

REFERENCES:

1.   Gibb-Clark, M., The Changing Face Of Mentoring;
        http://www.cybf.ca/insight/mentoring/articles/article.htm

2.   Ibid.

REWARD AND RECOGNITION:

46. WITH THANKS:
IDENTIFYING REWARD AND RECOGNITION ITEMS VALUED BY VARIOUS DEMOGRAPHIC GROUPS WITHIN WORK ORGANIZATIONS

 LEARNING OBJECTIVES:

1. To introduce you to the challenges of developing specialized reward and recognition packages for various demographic groups within the workforce.

2. To demonstrate the link between motivation theory and compensation practices.

TYPE OF EXERCISE:

Small group activities and class-wide discussions

RELATED CONCEPTS:

- Rewards and recognition
- Compensation
- Demographic groups in the workforce
- Career stages and development

 TIME: 50 minutes

The three career stage groups will typically require 20 minutes to review their interview data and to organize their findings into a class report. The class reports by career stage and debriefing will take another 15 minutes each.

BACKGROUND:

David Foot and Daniel Stoffman[1] have described the characteristics of the Canadian generation cohorts born in the twentieth century. By now, most of the World War I generation (born between 1915 and 1919), the Roaring Twenties generation (born between 1920 and 1929) and the relatively small Depression Baby generation (born between 1930 and 1939) have all retired from the workforce. The World War II babies (born between 1940 and 1946), a relatively larger cohort than the Depression Baby cohort before them, felt a competitive squeeze but managed to prosper overall. The next cohort, the Baby Boomers generation (born between 1947 and 1966), was notable for its shear size.

In 1959, at the height of the boom, 479 000 babies were born in Canada. This very high birth rate, coupled with large increases in immigration, produced a generation that formed one third of Canada's population in the mid 1990s. However, it is a mistake to consider the Baby Boomers as one large, unified demographic. Life has been more prosperous for the members of the leading edge of the baby boom than it has been for the so called Generation X (or Gen-X) group born between 1960 and 1966. Gen-Xers are the people who have had to compete with those just a few years older who have benefitted from the expansion in the 1970s and 1980s. The leading edge Baby Boomers occupy most of the higher rungs on the corporate ladder, blocking the way for the Gen-Xers. In fact, the Gen-Xers have had to cope with life-long overcrowding which has prompted them to become mistrustful of large institutions and which has taught them instead to become self-reliant. Many Gen-Xers have had to live with their parents well into adulthood because of low employment rates and the high cost of housing. What has made their lives even more complicated is conflict with their World War II generation parents who have been very successful themselves and do not understand why their children cannot pull themselves up by the bootstraps and get to work.

The late Baby Boom Gen-Xers were followed by the Baby Bust generation (born between 1967 and 1979). This comparatively smaller generation, especially its younger members, are enjoying brighter economic prospects than the Gen-Xers. Such prospects have freed the Baby Bust generation to be more idealistic than the cash-strapped Gen-Xers.

The Baby Boom Echo generation were born between 1980 and 1995. The front end of the Boom Echo group will most likely have more opportunities than the later-born Echos, known as Gen X-II. However, Gen X-II young people will have the understanding of their Gen-X parents who faced similar employment challenges.

The Millennium generation born between 1995 and 2010 is expected to be a relatively small cohort. This may well be another favoured generation faced with fewer competitive challenges than the two X generations before it.[2]

Understanding this pattern of boom and bust over the generations is important for HR professionals who are expected to develop meaningful and effective reward and recognition strategies that will appeal to members of the various generations at any given time in their work organizations. For example, the leading edge Baby Boomers like hierarchies and enjoy seeking promotions within them, work a standard nine-to-five work week and look forward to a comfortable retirement at age sixty-five or sooner. In contrast, the Gen-Xers are more computer literate than the older Boomers, work on contracts rather than in the full time jobs, dislike (or are at best are indifferent) to hierarchies and "expect to work until they die, but take long sabbaticals throughout.[3]

Don Tapscott has labeled the older Baby Busters, the Echo generation and the leading edge of the Millennium generation the Net Generation since "...it is the first to grow up surrounded by digital media."[4] Tapscott believes that the Net Generations' comfort with digital technology will be its defining feature. He describes the Net Generation as "...is exceptionally curious, self-reliant, contrarian, smart, focused, able to adapt, high in self-esteem, and has a global orientation."[5]

Aside from the influences of the demographic generation to which an employee belongs, a person's interests and reinforcers change as a function of career stage. There are three general career stages: early, middle and late. The early stage is characterized by the identification of critical career anchors which are the perceptions we have of our abilities, our values and the needs we hope to fulfill through work. In the middle stage, workers reevaluate their status as they face decreasing promotional opportunities and job alternatives. At this stage, an individual may choose to maintain the status quo, take advantage of career development interventions offered by their organizations or change careers entirely. Some people decide to start their own business. In the late stage, an individual is involved in planning for succession and for retirement.[6]

This exercise will give you the opportunity to explore the different HR strategies for reward and recognition that are most effective with different generations and at different career stages.

 MATERIALS NEEDED:

- One copy of the interview format and a consent form (as distributed by your instructor).
- One transparency sheet and one marker for each career stage group

PREASSIGNMENT STUDENT PREPARATION:

1. Your instructor will assign you to a group of three students. You will also be assigned one of the three career stages (early stage, middle stage and late stage). With your group members, identify someone you know who you believe is in your assigned work stage and seek permission from that person for an interview.

2. Before the interview, brainstorm rewards, recognition mechanisms, incentives, etc. that you expect someone in your assigned and career stage/generation would be likely to value. Write three additional questions for the interview format to "test your hunches" i.e., the importance of these rewards/recognition mechanisms/incentives to your interviewee.

3.   Conduct the interview using the format provided by your instructor (augmented with your own three questions (see step 2. above). Be sure to ask your interviewee to sign the Consent Form at the end of the interview. This will allow you to use the information you collect for discussion in class. The interview can be conducted on the telephone or in person.

PROCESS/INSTRUCTIONS:

1.   Your instructor will divide the class into three groups, one for each of the assigned career stages i.e., early stage, middle stage and later stage. Each interview group will join others in the class who were assigned the same career stage in the PREASSIGNMENT STUDENT PREPARATION section.

2.   In your larger career stage group, pool all the information gathered during the interviews to create a list of all the "rewards/recognition mechanisms/incentives" that would be most meaningful and effective for persons in this career stage/generation. Record this list on an overhead transparency sheet.

3.   Your instructor will ask each career stage/generation group to report in turn in the following order: late career stage, middle career stage and early career stage.

DEBRIEFING:

1.   What rewards/recognition mechanisms/incentives were mentioned most in the interviews by each career stage/generation?

2.   What are the rewards/recognition mechanisms/incentives that are most meaningful and effective for you? Do you think others who were born in your same "generation" would offer the same list as yours? Please explain your answer.

3.   How meaningful is the concept of demographic "generations" to HR professionals in work organizations? Are there any weaknesses in such an approach? Please explain.

4.   Speculate on the rewards/recognition mechanisms/incentives list for the Millennium generation as they pass through each of the three career stages.

5.   How would you expect the career stages differ between Canada (a country with mandatory retirement) and the United States (a country without mandatory retirement)?

FOLLOW-UP ACTIVITIES:

1.   Continue the research you have begun in this exercise by discussing with members of your family and friends about the rewards/recognition mechanisms/incentives that they value most in their work life.

2.   Do some extended research on the topic of mandatory versus non-mandatory retirement policies in three countries other than Canada and the United States.

REFERENCES:

1.   Foot, D.K. and Stoffman, D. (1996). *Boom, Bust & Echo: How to Profit from the Coming Demographic Shift*. Toronto: MacfarlaneWalter & Ross.

2.   Ibid.

3.   Bingham, R. and McCullough, M.(1998, November). Rebels with a business plan. *The Globe and Mail Report on Business Magazine,* pp. 77-88.

4.   Louder Echo: The Net Generation; http://www.growingupdigital.com/Lecho.html

5.   Ibid.

6.   Greenberg, J., Baron, R.A., Sales, C.A., and Owen, F.A. (1996). *Behaviour in Organizations*. Scarborough, Ontario: Prentice Hall Canada, pp. 211-215.

47. DIFFERENT STROKES FOR DIFFERENT OCCUPATIONAL GROUPS: DESIGNING SALIENT REWARDS AND RECOGNITION FOR INDIVIDUALS IN DIFFERENT OCCUPATIONAL GROUPS

 LEARNING OBJECTIVES:

1.   To identify salient financial and non-financial rewards and recognition components for individuals in different occupational groups.

2.   To investigate the reward and recognition strategies of contemporary Canadian organizations for different occupational groups.

TYPE OF EXERCISE:

Invited panel and class-wide discussion

RELATED CONCEPTS:

- Rewards and recognition
- Positive reinforcement
- Shaping
- Organizational behaviour modification
- Motivation
- Needs theories
- Compensation and benefits
- Recruitment and selection

 TIME: 45 minutes

The panel presentation and questions will require a maximum of 30 minutes. The debriefing will require an additional 15 minutes.

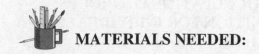 **MATERIALS NEEDED:**

- One copy of the "Rewards/Recognition Strategies Comparison/Contrast Sheet" (supplied by your instructor).

PREASSIGNMENT STUDENT PREPARATION:

1. For this exercise, your instructor will be inviting a panel of managers from some of the following different types of organizations: hospitals/nursing homes, call centres, retail sales and manufacturing to come to class and discuss financial and non-financial reward and recognition strategies used in their organizations. The target occupations will be some or all of the following: nurses, order takers (call centres), sales associates, and machine operators. To prepare for the class in which you will be listening to the panel, search the Internet or daily newspapers for job ads for the above named target occupations (and/or others identified by your instructor).

2. Speculate on the types of financial and non-financial rewards and recognition that might be currently in vogue in the various organizations and for the target occupations. Bring your notes to class.

3. Please answer the questions:

    - How much should and how can organizations tailor their reward and recognition strategies to suit the individual differences of employees?

    - How can organizations tailor their reward and recognition strategies to suit the individual differences of employees?

PROCESS/INSTRUCTIONS:

1. At the beginning of class (before the introduction of the panel), your instructor will hand out a worksheet on which you will be able to make notes during the panel presentation. Next, your instructor will ask each panelist to introduce herself or himself and give a brief profile of her/his organization and the related target occupation.

2. Your instructor will then ask the panelists to describe the financial and non-financial reward and recognition strategies used in their organizations for the different target occupational groups. Make notes on the worksheet given to you at the beginning of the class as the discussion progresses.

3. When all the panelists have made their presentations, you will be allowed to ask the panelists questions for a period of 10 minutes.

4. After the brief question period, the panelists will be thanked by the instructor and be excused from the class.

DEBRIEFING:

1. Were there any surprises for you in the panelists' information?

2. What were the most salient types of reward and recognition for each occupational group? Which needs were the different strategies targeting?

3. How aware did the panelists seem to be about individual differences within each occupational group? Give examples of reward and recognition strategies mentioned by the panelists that you felt accounted for individual differences and others that you felt ignored individual differences.

4. Of all the financial and non-financial rewards and recognition strategies mentioned which appealed the most to you? The least to you? Please explain your answers.

FOLLOW-UP ACTIVITIES:

1. Write a class letter to the panelists thanking them for sharing their time and information with you.

2. Write a job ad for each of the target occupation in which you point out the potential rewards and recognition in "your organization".

HEALTH AND SAFETY

48. SHOW ME THE HEALTH PROMO: PROMOTING WORKPLACE HEALTH

 LEARNING OBJECTIVES:

1.   To increase your awareness of Health Canada's Workplace Health System.

2.   To give you experience in designing a workplace health promotion plan.

TYPE OF EXERCISE:

Small group activities and class-wide discussion

RELATED CONCEPTS:

*   Health and safety
*   Stress
*   Recruitment and selection
*   Retention of employees

 TIME: 65 minutes (assuming 5 groups)

Small groups will be given 10 minutes each in which to present their workplace health promotion plans. The vote will take 5 minutes. The debriefing will require another 10 minutes.

BACKGROUND:

Health Canada has determined that Canadian workers spend 60% of their waking time in the workplace. The type of work and the work environment can have a significant impact on the health of workers. Health Canada's Workplace Health System is designed, not just to prevent illness, but to promote health. "To be healthy means to be able to cope with and adapt to the

211

changes going on around us; health refers not only to our physical condition, but also to our state of mental and social well-being."[1]

Health Canada's System focuses on three areas of work life: the environment (both physical and psychosocial) in which workers live at home and at work, personal resources including employees' empowerment and social support, and health practices such as exercise, substance abuse, diet and sleeping habits. Health Canada believes that, if organizations are to be successful in promoting worker health, all three areas must be included must be addressed. Stress management, counselling, financial planning and literacy classes should all be included in a comprehensive workplace health promotion plan.[2]

This exercise will encourage you to examine the elements that should be included in a workplace health promotion program.

PREASSIGNMENT STUDENT PREPARATION:

1.   Before the class in which you will be completing this exercise, visit Health Canada's Work Place Health site (http://www.hc-sc.gc.ca/hppb/ahi/workplace/pube/workplacehealth/system2.htm). Investigate the web site's resources for HR professionals.

2.   Also, before the class in which you will be completing this exercise, your instructor will divide the class into small groups. Each group will also be assigned a business sector on which to focus this exercise. After reviewing the Health Canada web site, work with your group colleagues to design any two of the following: a poster, a brochure, an overhead transparency, an electronic presentation to present your group's vision of the ideal workplace health promotion program for your assigned work sector. Target your health promotion advertising strategy at potential new employees you hope to attract to join your company. If you need audio visual equipment to support your presentation beyond that which is always available in your classroom, please draw this to the attention of your instructor several days before your presentation to the class.

PROCESS/INSTRUCTIONS:

1.   Each group will be given 10 minutes to display and describe its health promotion strategy to the class. Start your presentation by describing the business sector on which you were focusing and then display your print or electronic presentation. Remember that this program is an important way for your company to attract talented new employees so do make your presentation clear and compelling.

2.   At the end of all the presentations your instructor will ask the class to vote by a show of hands for the health promotion program that would be most appealing to them as a prospective employee.

DEBRIEFING:

1. Discuss how important health promotion opportunities are to you in your employment decision making process.

2. Discuss what elements of the health promotion plans discussed in class were of most importance to you.

FOLLOW-UP ACTIVITIES:

1. Visit company web sites (for example, Husky Injection Molding at http://www.husky.on.ca) to review corporate health promotion strategies.

2. Invite to your class your local medical officer of health, a mental health professional and an HR professional to form a panel to answer questions about workplace health promotion.

REFERENCES:

1. Workplace Health System: An Overview, Creating A Healthy Workplace; http://www.hc-sc.gc.ca/hppb/ahi/workplace/pube/workplacehealth/system2.htm

2. Ibid.

49. FEELING SAFE AT WORK:
WORKPLACE VIOLENCE RISK ASSESSMENT

 LEARNING OBJECTIVES:

1.   To make you aware of the growing problem of workplace violence.

2.   To give you experience in planning a workplace risk assessment.

TYPE OF EXERCISE:

Small group activities and class-wide discussion

RELATED CONCEPTS:

*   Workplace violence
*   Health and safety

 TIME: 40 Minutes

It will take the discussion pairs approximately 30 minutes to identify the assessment categories, fill in specific assessment areas under each category and devise assessment strategies for each area. Debriefing will require an additional 10 minutes.

BACKGROUND:

Workplace violence is a pressing concern for HR professionals in all work settings. The Federal Bureau of Investigation statistics indicate that violence in the workplace "is the number one growing homicide in the United States."[1] Canada has also had its share of workplace violence. While some workplaces, such as prisons, have more obvious risks than others, every workplace has the potential for violence. HR professionals who feel inappropriately safe will put themselves and their colleagues at increased risk.

The regulations of the Workers' Compensation Board of British Columbia [2] requires that a risk assessment be conducted in any work setting that has experienced violence or where there has been violence in a similar workplace. Whether or not regulations in your area require this kind of assessment, it is always a worthwhile undertaking. The elements of a risk assessment include, first, an examination of the nature of interactions among workers and between workers and the public. Is money changing hands? Are substances such as drugs or alcohol involved in these transactions? Second, the assessment must examine the personal, educational and experiential attributes of both workers and consumers which may contribute to violence. Third, the assessment must include an examination of the nature of the work environment. Does lighting promote safety? Are there enough exits or are staff trapped in their work spaces? Is there a security system in place? Do the hours of operation contribute to staff or consumer risk? Finally, the assessment must include an analysis of the history of violence in the workplace and in other similar workplaces.[3]

This exercise will help you to develop a heightened awareness of workplace violence issues.

 MATERIALS NEEDED:

- One sheet of flip chart paper and one marker for each small group
- One roll of masking tape

PREASSIGNMENT STUDENT PREPARATION:

Before the class in which you will be completing this exercise, search the Internet to discover your province's standards for workplace risk assessment. The best web site to start with is the Human Resources Development Canada's Human Resource Office for Employers web site (http://www.hroe.org/). Here you will find links to sites all across Canada.

PROCESS/INSTRUCTIONS:

1. Your instructor will divide the class into small groups. Your instructor will assign you a type of workplace for which you will develop your risk assessment.

2. Within your small group, review the regulations and other material you gathered during your Internet search on workplace risk assessment. On the left side of a sheet of flip chart paper, make a master list of the general categories that should be covered in your risk assessment. Leave a 15 cm. space between categories. Print the type of workplace on the top of the paper.

3.　　　Brainstorm all the specific risk factors in each category from Step 2. above which relate to your assigned type of workplace. On the flip chart paper, under each category, list as many potential risk factors as you can. Feel free to add new categories to the bottom of your original list.

4.　　　On the right side of the flip chart paper, identify how you would assess the level of risk in each area you listed.

5.　　　Your instructor will ask each group to report on your work on risk assessment to the class.

DEBRIEFING:

1.　　　Reflect on a time that you felt unsafe at work or at school. What was the source of your discomfort? What strategies should the organization have taken in that setting to insure your safety?

2.　　　Compare the assessment strategies recommended by each group in your class. What changes would you make to your list based on the ideas of your colleagues?

FOLLOW-UP ACTIVITIES:

1.　　　Revisit the Human Resources Office For Employers web site and research workplace risk assessment for provinces other than your own. Notice the similarities and differences in the workplace violence regulations across the country.

2.   As you visit your local mall, doctor's office, variety store, grocery store or any other local organization, notice the security measures that are in place. From your perspective as a visitor, what additional measures should be taken to insure the safety of workers in these organizations?

REFERENCES:

1.   Robinson, J.L. (1996). 10 Facts Every Employer Should Know About Workplace Violence: It May Save Your Life, Institute of Workplace Violence Prevention; http://www.smartbiz.com/sbs/columns/robin1.htm

2.   Preventing workplace violence; http://www.wcb.bc.ca/resmat/pubs/violence.htm

3.   Ibid.

50. CHECKING OUT MY SAFEGUARDS: WORKPLACE VIOLENCE PREVENTION PROGRAM

 LEARNING OBJECTIVES:

1.   To sensitize you to the issue of workplace violence.

2.   To give you experience assessing a workplace violence prevention program.

TYPE OF EXERCISE:

Small group activities and class-wide discussion

RELATED CONCEPTS:

*   Health and Safety
*   Workplace violence
*   HR development

 TIME: 35 minutes

The small groups typically will require 15 minutes to determine the greatest two strengths and weaknesses in your school's workplace violence prevention program. The cumulative chalkboard list of strengths and weaknesses will take 10 minutes. The debriefing will require an additional 10 minutes.

BACKGROUND:

The prevention of workplace violence is an important part of every organization's Health and Safety Program.[1] The causes of workplace violence are many and varied. They include pressure from downsizing, growth in the use of technology, mergers, high unemployment, employees who have experienced abuse in their own lives and violence as an increasing factor in society at large. Organizational factors that can increase the likelihood of workplace violence include rifts between management and workers, an authoritarian management style and the lack of an adequate mechanism for the resolution of grievances.[2] While it is tempting to think "It will never

218

happen here", all HR professionals must be prepared to address the potential for workplace violence.

The Nova Scotia Department of Human Resources [3] emphasizes, among other measures, the importance of all employees' being familiar with their organization's safety plans. It also recommends the prominent posting of emergency numbers and the ready availability of first aid kits. These are key safety features in all workplaces. According to the Workers' Compensation Board of British Columbia, a workplace violence prevention program should include the following elements: a written policy, regular risk assessments, prevention procedures, worker and supervisor training, incident reporting and investigation, incident follow-up, and program review.[4]

This exercise will give you experience in planning a workplace violence prevention program.

PREASSIGNMENT STUDENT PREPARATION:

Before the class in which you will be completing this exercise, visit your college or university's web site and gather information from your student union about the strategies your institution uses to insure the safety of its students and staff. Take note of the methods your college or university administration and your student union use to inform faculty, staff, and students about the safeguards available to them. Also take note of the strategies used to evaluate the effectiveness of the violence prevention program.

PROCESS/INSTRUCTIONS:

1. Your instructor will divide the class into four person discussion groups. In your group, identify the strengths and weaknesses of your college or university's workplace violence plan.

2. After a thorough discussion of the strengths and weaknesses you identified in Step 1. above, choose the greatest two strengths and greatest two weaknesses in your college or university's workplace violence plan.

3. Your instructor will divide the chalkboard into a "Strengths" section and a "Weaknesses" section. When your instructor signals the end of the small group discussion time, add your group's greatest two strengths and greatest two weaknesses to the class list on the chalkboard.

4. Your instructor will facilitate your review of the chalkboard list of strengths and weaknesses.

DEBRIEFING:

1. Think back on the orientation you experienced as a first year student in your college or university. What training did you receive in violence prevention?

2. If you were on the orientation committee, how would you change the manner in which first year students are informed about violence prevention?

3. Consider the special challenges of people in charge of college and residences. Develop a violence prevention program for the residences in your school.

FOLLOW-UP ACTIVITIES:

1. As a class, write a memo to your college or university's HR department to outline the strengths and weaknesses your class has identified in your school's workplace violence prevention plan.

2. Examine the workplace violence prevention program of any two colleges or universities (or one of each) besides your own.

REFERENCES:

1. Preventing workplace violence; http://www.wcb.bc.ca/resmat/pubs/violence.htm

2. Robinson, J.L. (1996). 10 Facts Every Employer Should Know About Workplace Violence: It May Save Your Life, Institute of Workplace Violence Prevention; http://www.smartbiz.com/sbs/columns/robin1.htm

3. Personal Safety in the Workplace; http://www.gov.ns.ca/humr/info/womensaf.htm

4. Preventing workplace violence; ibid.

PART 4

BUILDING EMPLOYEE COMMITMENT

WORK/LIFE BALANCE

51. GIVE US A BREAK, PLEASE: DEVELOPING FAMILY-FRIENDLY PROGRAMS AT WORK

 LEARNING OBJECTIVES:

1. To increase your awareness of the impact of family care pressures on workers.

2. To give you experience planning programs that promote a family friendly workplace.

TYPE OF EXERCISE:

Group Internet research, small group activities and class-wide discussion

RELATED CONCEPTS:

*   Benefits
*   Stress
*   HR strategy

 TIME: 50 minutes

The small group discussion and development of the accommodation plan will typically require 25 minutes. The presentation of accommodation plans to the class will take approximately 15 minutes. The debriefing will require an additional 10 minutes.

BACKGROUND:

Elder care, child care, overtime, deadlines, paying bills, house cleaning, shopping - the list of responsibilities faced by today's worker is endless. In the bad old days companies saw anything that was not directly related to company business as being irrelevant to work life. Increasingly companies are realizing that if they want the best work from their employees they have to provide ways to help them reduce the stress from other areas of life.

This exercise will sensitize you to some of the challenging issues facing employees today and the ways in which HR professionals can respond.

 ## MATERIALS NEEDED:

- One sheet of flip chart paper and a marker for each small group
- One roll of masking tape

PREASSIGNMENT STUDENT PREPARATION:

1. Pretend that your classroom is the head office of a medium-sized national insurance company. Your instructor will divide "the office" into four groups. One group will be asked to play the role of the company's HR department which has been charged with the responsibility for developing programs to make the company more family-friendly. The other three groups will represent employees who share a concern which could be addressed through work-family accommodation programs. These groups will include: a group that includes middle-aged employees who have aging parents for whom they are responsible, a group of dual income working parents who have young children, and a group of parents who have children who have special needs (such as medical or learning concerns) that require regular meetings with specialists.

2. Before the class in which family-friendly programs are to be discussed, meet with your head office group. For the employee groups, your task is to research the special concerns of your focus. The elder care group may wish to start the search with Elderweb (http://www.elderweb.com); the dual income parents may wish to start the search with No Work, No Life, No Kidding (http://www.fastcompany.com/online/07/138nonono.html) and the group focusing on parents who have children with special needs may wish to start the search with KidSource Online - Health: Diseases, Disorders, Illnesses and Medical Problems (http://www.kidsource.com/kidsource/pages/health.diseases.html) or Disability-Related Sites on the World Wide Web (http://thearc.org/misc/disinkin.html#lists). Gather information from the Internet, newspapers, magazines and any other sources to which you have access to insure that you have a good understanding of the kinds of challenges faced by employees with these various caregiving responsibilities. Each group will develop a list of accommodations that would be necessary to help employees facing these challenges to be most effective on the job. Bring your group's list to class.

3.   The HR group will also meet before the class in which family-friendly workplaces are discussed. The HR group's task is to gather information on family-friendly programs that are of assistance to employees who face the caregiving responsibilities faced by the other three groups in your class. You may wish to start your search with Work-Life Benefits Reap Business Benefits (http://www.shrm.org/hrmagazine/articles/0697flex.htm) or Work/Life Issues (http://www.shrm.org/hrlinks/family.htm). Make a list of the accommodations that are appropriate for the challenges facing the other three class groups. Bring this list to class.

PROCESS/INSTRUCTIONS:

1.   The three employee groups will sit together. Your instructor will distribute the HR group among the other three employee groups. The task of each employee group with the HR representatives is to plan one program that will address an issue of major concern to employees facing the challenge which you researched. The HR representatives in each group will chair the group. The plan should be written on the flip chart paper provided by your instructor and should include: a description of the concern that the plan will address, a list of resources that will be needed to support the plan and a description of the benefits the plan will produce for employees and for the company. Tape the group's completed accommodation plan to a wall in the classroom.

2.   The HR representatives from each group will present the accommodation plans to the class.

DEBRIEFING:

1.   Reflect on the unique challenges facing employees who have elder care, child care and special needs care responsibilities. What additional physical and emotional challenges do you expect that people facing these caregiving challenges would have in their own lives?

2.   As a future HR professional, how has the experience of learning about the challenges facing family caregivers changed your approach to the development of benefits programs?

FOLLOW-UP ACTIVITIES:

1.   Interview professional caregivers in services for seniors, for children and for children who have special needs. Gather from them information concerning the special challenges they encounter in meeting the needs of the people for whom they provide services. Also ask these caregivers about the concerns they have for family members of their clients.

2.   Invite to your class an HR professional who specializes in developing family-friendly programs. Ask this person to discuss the process his/her company uses to determine which programs will be most useful.

52. NOBODY EVER SAID BEING A SINGLE PARENT WAS EASY: AN INVESTIGATION INTO ISSUES OF SINGLE PARENT ACCOMMODATION

 **LEARNING OBJECTIVES:**

1. To highlight some of the potential issues facing single parent families.

2. To identify organizational strategies to accommodate the special needs of single parents.

3. To highlight potential equity issues in accommodating for the needs of single parents.

TYPE OF EXERCISE:

Individual Internet research, small group activities and class-wide discussion

RELATED CONCEPTS:

*   Single parent accommodation
*   Stress
*   Diversity

 TIME: 60 minutes

The reading of the scenario, review of Internet resources, and the listing of interventions will typically require 25 minutes. The formulation of recommendations will require 10 minutes. The presentations and voting will require 15 minutes. The debriefing will take an additional 10 minutes.

BACKGROUND:

The challenge of balancing work and family life pressures is an increasingly important issue for Human resource professionals. This challenge is especially acute for single parents who are faced with providing the necessities of life for themselves and their children while meeting the demands of the workplace. The Canadian organization Voices for Children reports that "single

227

parents experience less choice to reduce work hours to parent-time than other parents.[1] With this pressure to work full time, the single parents face enormous stress juggling all the responsibilities they bear.

This exercise will sensitize you to the crushing pressures faced by single parents in the workforce and will give you experience developing a sample accommodation plan for a single parent.

 MATERIALS NEEDED:

- Three sheets of flip chart paper and one marker for each small group
- One roll of masking tape

PREASSIGNMENT STUDENT PREPARATION:

Before the class in which you will be completing this exercise, compile a resource file of single parent friendly work practices. Several web sites may be used as a good starting point for this research. The Voice for Children site entitled: Work and Family-Friendly Intiatives (http://www. Voices for children.org/factsheet/background2-3.htm) gives statistics on work-family stresses in Canada and details strategies which companies can take to address these issues. The Work And Family Newsbrief site (http://www.workfamily.com) includes links to a variety of sites focusing on a variety of issues related to your topic. You may also find it helpful to check your local and national newspapers and popular business magazines for stories about how single parents are balancing the pressures of work and family life. Bring the materials you gather to class.

PROCESS/INSTRUCTIONS:

1. Your instructor will divide the class into same gender three-person groups. Within your group, review the following scenario:

    Kristen Craig is a 37 year old manager who was recently hired by your firm two years ago, a large Canadian trust company based in Toronto. Based on her superb reputation as a credit manager with a large bank in Montreal, you aggressively recruited her to join your company. She was very excited about her career potential with your organization, since she felt the bank was moving very slowly in promoting women. Kristen is considered to have very high potential.

    When she was hired it was anticipated that she would be promoted to Director within 36 months. In fact, her performance has exceeded your company's expectations and, last week, the Executive Committee called her in to announce her promotion. Contrary to expectations, Kristen promptly declined the promotion. The Executive Vice President (EVP) was very upset. The EVP has asked you, the Vice President of Human Resources, to speak with Kristen to find out why she is declining this offer and to try to convince her to take it.

Kristen is a single mother of two. When she accepted the position with your company, she had relocated to Toronto from her hometown of Montreal (with a full relocation package). Her children are 5 and 9 years of age. Kristen is under considerable stress at the moment. Both of her children miss Kristen's family in Montreal. Her nine year old son, Aaron, is having trouble in school. Sarah, her five year old daughter, cries when she leaves for work and often is in bed by the time Kristen gets home at night. Kristen feels undersupported, to say the least, as a single mother. She claims that the banks, such as the one she worked for in Montreal, are much more progressive in supporting individuals in her circumstances.

Currently she is working 10-12 hours a day and often misses dinner with her children. She also feels pressured to be in the office by 7:00 a.m. (Her boss has early morning coffee meetings at 7:30 a.m. daily) and her nanny must see her children off to school. Because of the pressure in her work unit, she has been unable to take a vacation since joining the company. Her children have spent holidays with their grandparents, aunts and uncles in Montreal and their father, Ben, who lives in Calgary.

When you meet with Kristen, as asked by the EVP, you notice how tired and drawn she looks. She tells you that loves her job. She says that she has never felt so professionally rewarded or challenged. She is distraught over having to decline the promotion and is equally upset over the time that she has missed with her children since taking the job with your company. She tells you that she has been feeling so torn between her job and parenting responsibilities that she is considering leaving the company. Her old bank has called her and wants her to return to her former job in Montreal where her family and friends can help her to raise the children and where she has family-friendly benefits that allow her to spend more time with her children.

You are very worried about losing Kristen's valuable contribution to your company. You call the EVP and suggest that you would like to make a recommendation about how your firm might address this situation. The EVP has strongly encouraged you to think about this as an HR imperative and wants both short and long term recommendations to address this issue not only for Kristen but for all single parents in the company.

2. Review the resources that you and your group members of your group gathered in preparation for this exercise. Make a list of the categories of interventions that companies have used and consider how these may relate to the issues that are of concern to Kristen.

3. Divide each of the three sheets of flip chart paper (supplied by your instructor) into thirds by drawing two lines across the sheet. On each of the sheets, list one recommendation for

your EVP concerning a program your company could undertake to support single parents working for your firm. In the top third of each sheet, write a brief description of the program. In the middle third of each sheet list the estimated human, equipment and financial resources that would be necessary to support the program. In the bottom third of the sheet, list the benefits that your group expects would accrue to employees and to the firm if the program was put into operation.

4. Elect one member of your group to be the person responsible for making the presentation to the EVP. All class members who are not presenting will assume the role of the EVP. Your instructor will ask each group in turn to present. Each group will post its sheets on the chalkboard walls of your classroom after the presentation.

5. After all presentations have been made your instructor will ask class members to move around the classroom and vote on their three favourite proposals by putting a check mark in the upper right hand corner of their three chosen sheets. Your instructor will tally the votes and announce the winners.

DEBRIEFING:

1. What themes were similar among the recommendations made by the various groups in your class?

2. What risks may be associated with introducing accommodation strategies for certain demographic groups?

3.   If you were a single parent like Kristen in the case, what accommodations would you look for in a new employment opportunity?

FOLLOW-UP ACTIVITIES:

1.   Interview people you know who are working single parents. What accommodations have been provided in their workplaces? What accommodations have been most helpful for them? How have these accommodations changed their lives? What additional accommodations would they like to have introduced in their workplaces?

2.   Visit the web sites of major Canadian banks, high tech firms, retail chains, government agencies, utilities and industries. Notice whether they advertise aspects of their workplace that are family friendly.

REFERENCE:

1.   Work and Family-Friendly Initiatives;
      http://www.voices4children.org/factsheet/background2-3.htm

COMMUNICATION

53. JUST TOUCHING BASE:
CORPORATE NEWSLETTERS AS PART OF COMMUNICATION STRATEGY

 LEARNING OBJECTIVES:

1. To introduce you to different types of employee newsletters.

2. To give you experience in analyzing the content, purpose and effectiveness of company newsletters.

3. To help you to develop skills in the construction of a company newsletter.

TYPE OF EXERCISE:

Group Internet research, small group activities and class-wide discussion

RELATED CONCEPTS:

-   HR strategy
-   Employee relations
-   Communication
-   Culture

TIME: 30 minutes

Small groups will typically require 20 minutes to review all the newsletters and to discuss the rewards and challenges. The debriefing will take an additional 10 minutes.

BACKGROUND:

Employee newsletters are an effective way to build corporate culture, increase awareness of organizational strategy and mission, and encourage employee involvement in corporate activities. Often HR has the responsibility for developing a corporate employee communication strategy. Newsletters can be a very useful communication tool.

This exercise will give you the opportunity to examine different approaches to newsletter writing and to develop a newsletter for the staff of your business school.

PREASSIGNMENT STUDENT PREPARATION:

1.   Your instructor will divide the class into small groups. Your first task is to search the Internet for examples of company newsletters. Please start at the CompanyNewsletters.com web pages entitled: Ten Tips to Make Sure Your Company Newsletter Gets Read, Not Tossed (http://www.companynewsletters.com/newsread.htm) and How to Use an Employee Newsletter to Help Workers Cope with a Corporate Downsizing, Merger or Acquisition http://www.companynewsletters.com/downsize.htm). These and connected sites will give you insight into the process of designing a newsletter. You may also find it helpful to visit sample newsletter sites including the following:

   - Petrochemical Corporation of Singapore (Private) Limited's newsletter site (http://www.pcs.com.sg/sub08.htm),
   - Medical Center Information Systems department's newsletter at Duke University (http://scalos.mc.duke.edu/orientation/newsletter.html),
   - Lear Corporation's newsletter (http://www.lear.com/c/cl.htm),
   - GS Electric's newsletter (http://www.gselectric.com/newsletters/9709nl.htm),
   - City of Frederick's newsletter (http://www.cityoffrederick.com/hrd/cs-head.htm).

2.   Notice the kinds of information that are included in a typical company newsletter:

   - Business updates
   - Employee information
   - Company events
   - Human Resource programs
   - Other Information

3.   Using the list your group develops from the step 2. above, identify the kinds of activities that involve students entering your College or University Faculty of Business which could be included in a Faculty of Business newsletter.

4.   Within your group, develop a sample newsletter with enough copies to share with your class. This newsletter should be a minimum of two pages in length. It should be developed bearing in mind the guidelines suggested in the CompanyNewsletters.com is Ten Tips web site (http://www.companynewsletters.com/newsread.htm).

PROCESS/INSTRUCTIONS:

1.   Bring copies of your sample newsletter to class. Your instructor will invite you to distribute these to your class colleagues. Within your work group, review the newsletters developed by your colleagues. Notice the similarities and differences among the newsletters.

2.   As a class, discuss the rewards in and challenges of developing your newsletter.

DEBRIEFING:

1.   Discuss the way in which your newsletter could be expanded to include staff and faculty activities that take place in your Faculty of Business or across your whole College or University Campus.

2.   What do the newsletters tell you about the student culture in your Faculty of Business?

3.   What are the benefits for a large corporation in having a quality newsletter? What are the costs of such a newsletter?

FOLLOW-UP ACTIVITIES:

1.   Invite a panel of staff from your business school to meet with your class to give you ideas about what should be included in a staff newsletter.

2.   Interview the editor of your college's or university's faculty and staff newsletter(s) to learn how decisions are made about the content and format of the publication(s). Also ask the editor about the goals he/she has for the newsletter.

54. THIS IS ME LEAVING!:
UNDERSTANDING AND DEVELOPING EXIT INTERVIEWS

 LEARNING OBJECTIVES:

1.   To teach you the "whys" and "hows" of the HR tool known as the exit interview.

2.   To give you an opportunity to develop, conduct and follow-up on an exit interview.

3.   To give you insight into the enormous costs associated with employee turnover.

4.   To stimulate your thinking on different HR strategies and methodologies for reversing turnover in a given organization.

TYPE OF EXERCISE:

Small group activities, role play and class-wide discussion

RELATED CONCEPTS:

- Employee turnover and associated costs
- Motivation
- Job satisfaction
- HR strategy
- HR development
- Recruitment and selection
- Coaching
- Organizational climate
- Organizational change and development

 TIME: 40 minutes

Small groups will typically require about 10 minutes to devise a list of reasons for leaving and to share them with the rest of the class. The role play session and the debriefing will take another 15 minutes each.

BACKGROUND:

Employee turnover is a costly proposition for organizations in so many ways. The costs of recruitment, selection, training and development are gargantuan. When a valuable employee leaves the organization, not only does the organization lose its expensive investment in human capital, but also it is forced to repeat that investment cycle when it fills the vacancy with a new-hire.

HR can play a valuable role in understanding turnover in a given organization by unearthing and analyzing its root causes, tracking trends, recommending changes to the organization's HR strategy for reversing turnover and enhancing the retention rate of valuable employees and coaching the organization's managers. HR professionals make excellent use of a tool known as the exit interview, "a conversation with departing employees to learn their opinions of the employer, managers, policies, and other aspects of employment with the organization, and reason(s) for leaving".[1]

This exercise will help you gain a deeper understanding of the issues and costs involved in employee turnover. Further, you will gain a working knowledge of the exit interview as a valuable HR tool.

 MATERIALS NEEDED:

- One sheet of flip paper and one marker for each small group
- One roll of masking tape

PROCESS/INSTRUCTIONS:

1. Your instructor will ask if anyone in the class has either conducted an exit interview or been interviewed as part of his/her departure from an organization. Your instructor will then ask these persons to share a brief summary of their exit experiences and will ask that the name of any organization not be mentioned in class.

2. Your instructor will divide the class into five-person groups. Within your group, appoint one person to be the recorder. First, brainstorm a list of reasons why employees (assume a non-manager) might leave an organization. Your recorder will keep track of your ideas. Next, revisit this list with a view to rating the level of sensitivity of each item for an exiting employee who is being interviewed as she/he leaves an organization. Your recorder will read each item and ask the group to agree on one of the following ratings for that item: "HS/S": a mixture of highly sensitive reasons for leaving, (not likely to be revealed in an exit interview) and quite sensitive reasons (but may be revealed if there is a level of trust established between the HR interviewer and the interviewee) or "NS": not sensitive (likely to be revealed in an exit interview even if the trust level is not high between the HR interviewer and the interviewee).

3. Your instructor will ask the recorders in round robin fashion to read a sampling of the reasons for leaving from each "sensitivity" ranking starting with those reasons labeled HS/S and moving to the NS list. Your instructor will record a list of reasons from each ranking category on the chalkboard.

4. Please read the following scenario about exiting employee, Carla Martinez:

    Carla has handed in her resignation from her job as a senior systems engineer and will move to another company in two weeks. She is known across your company as a person with tremendous potential and has been a top performer since she came to your high tech organization eight years ago. Carla's department manager has lost two other senior people from his group in the last month.

5. In your small group, decide on what type of information you (an HR professional) should attempt to secure during your upcoming exit interview with Carla. Reach consensus on the three best questions to ask Carla. Your recorder will write these on a sheet of flip chart paper. Your instructor will ask the recorders to post these flip chart sheets on the walls of the classroom.

6. Your instructor will choose two students from the class as a whole to role play the exit interview. One student will take the role of the HR professional conducting the exit interview. (Your instructor will give additional information to the "interviewer".) The interviewer will select one question from each group's list of questions and will prepare a couple questions of his/her own. The other student will take the role of Carla. ("Carla" will be given some further information by your instructor.) After a few minutes of preparation, the "interviewer" will invite Carla into his/her office and will conduct the interview.

DEBRIEFING:

1. What were the types of questions which revealed the most information during the interview? Be sure to explain your answer.

2. What implications does the information revealed by Carla have for the company she is leaving?

3. What were the strengths of exit interviews conducted in class? What might have been done differently?

4. What are the costs involved in losing Carla and other top performers like her?

5. What are the strengths of the exit interview as an HR tool? Its weaknesses? Please explain your answers.

6. What should an HR interviewer do with the data from an exit interview? What should the interviewer not do with this data?

7. If Carla gave her permission to the HR interviewer to act on certain information she revealed during the interview, what changes would you recommend to department managers to stop your top performers such as Carla from leaving?

FOLLOW-UP ACTIVITIES:

1. Write a memo to the department managers (including Carla's) inviting them to sit down with you to discuss some ideas for stemming the tide of top performers from your company.

2. Draw up a list of questions which you think a professor who is leaving your business school should be asked in an exit interview. Who should conduct this interview?

REFERENCE:

1. Dessler, G., Cole, N.D. and Sutherland, V. (199). *Human Resources Management In Canada*. Canadian Seventh Edition. Scarborourgh, Ont: Prentice Hall Canada, p. 63.